RETAIL MANAGEMENT

Peter Ronald Fleming

For a complete list of Management Books 2000 titles, visit our website at www.mb2000.com

Text originally published as 'Managing Retail Sales'

First published in 2004 by Management Books 2000 Ltd

This new edition published in 2007 by Management Books 2000 Ltd
Forge House, Limes Road
Kemble, Cirencester
Gloucestershire, GL7 6AD, UK
Tel: 0044 (0) 1285 771441
Fax: 0044 (0) 1285 771055
E-mail: mb2000@btconnect.com
Web: www.mb2000.com

Printed and bound in Great Britain by4edge Ltd of Hockley, Essex - www.4edge.co.uk

British Library Cataloguing in Publication Data is available

ISBN 9781852525538

Foreword

Managing a retail business becomes more demanding year-by-year as trading conditions provide turbulence and unforeseen demands. However, the professional company – with consistent policies, and plans for achieving them – must provide a framework for line managers to carry out their roles successfully.

This is always made easier with the right training, coaching, planned experience and self-development – all factors which can be costly in money, effort and time – but still vital. The bssa contributes a valuable service to the Industry by helping with all these development initiatives and Peter Fleming's most recent book is the latest example of this.

I welcome *Retail Management* because it will help both newly-appointed and experienced Department and Branch managers improve their skills in:

- leading and motivating their sales teams and
- managing their part of the retailing business.

I wish all readers success in applying the principles in their sectors and in achieving continuing personal and business growth.

Peter Still

Managing Director, John Lewis, Oxford Street
and President of the Oxford Street Association

Author's Note

This book lays out a 'menu' from which the skilled manager can select those approaches and skills which can be developed and exploited in their particular business. Real competitive advantage will come from skilful application of the principles outlined. In this respect I would like to draw your attention also to the training workshops offered by the bssa, which are specifically designed to help participants to apply these principles in practice. We hope that the book will provoke a greater recognition of the importance of seeking this kind of help. This is what the bssa is for – and a full range of help is readily available.

I would like to take this opportunity of thanking all those who have helped us with the various case histories and illustrations - research for this book has covered ground from Kingston to Kuala Lumpur and experience is a great teacher! Thanks are due to the innumerable managers and other participants on past Workshops whose questions and experiences have helped shape the text.

The Management Books 2000 team has also helped us in the presentation of the contents and, once again, Peter King's acute illustrations have helped to lighten the text!

I hope that you enjoy reading the book and look forward to the possibility of meeting you on a Management Workshop in the near future.

Peter Fleming
PFA International
Maple House, 33 Owl Way,
Hartford, Cambridgeshire PE29 1YZ
Tel: 0870-3500878

Contents

1

What You Will Be Able to Achieve from this Book

1. Introduction

This book has been written with line managers in mind (Branch or Department Sales Managers, whose main accountability is to achieve targets agreed by more senior managers in the organisation).

Additionally, it will have application to more senior executives who wish to review the manager training and customer care programmes of their organisations – or consider instituting new ones. Our aim has been to provoke serious thought and action about the most important – but also vulnerable – area of the business: service to customers.

As with our 'sister' book, *'Retail Selling – How to Achieve Maximum Sales'*, this book aims to redefine theory and, through the practical tips and case histories, we believe it will have considerable value and application for sales managers everywhere.

There is a significant difference in management between the things we know about and those that we put into practice! This book is intended to enable the reader to put the principles into practice. Two factors will help this process:

- the Assignments which appear in each chapter
- attending a Management Workshop at which the motivating elements and skills can be explored in greater depth.

Nothing is ever quite as easy as it sounds or first appears. Service industries in the UK have had a 'patchy' image in recent decades – and have been seen by many as the 'also-rans' for careers and quality standards. In many cases this is quite unjustifiable; but it is still easy to pick out businesses with tarnished images, with poor quality merchandise and even more indifferent service. These firms do considerable disservice to themselves – as well as quite a lot of harm to the overall reputation of an exceedingly hard-working industry! Perhaps this book will help correct some of these situations and lead to a general lifting of standards – across the board. After all, from the customer's viewpoint, the industry is only as good as the last 'sale' – its service quality – and the durability and 'image' of the product or service purchased. And this is a **key learning point**:

All managers have a duty to ensure that the worst examples of standards cannot be witnessed on 'their' premises.

It has often been said that, if the best quality staff are recruited, then the business will never have a serious problem with customer service. There are two problems with this belief.

- Managers are often not in a position to afford the best applicants – the budget may not run to them.
- The daily 'grind' of customer service can reduce the motivation and enthusiasm even of 'saints', without constant managerial support and coaching behind them!

Good customer service may be easier to install and maintain when all staff have been brought up 'properly' and have a good understanding of what constitutes good manners, but good service is more than just the application of 'common sense'! Every business needs to establish the level of service which it wishes to be given to its customers, as part of its overall marketing plan; and then train and support all staff to match this standard.

Sales Managers must have a key role in helping to define customer service training plans and in implementing them!

2. 'Hard' v. 'soft' skills

In recent years there has been an unhealthy disregard for the importance of 'softer' people skills in business. Customer service may be regarded as one of the easier areas to target for financial cuts and, when budgets are tough, training – and other 'people-centred' initiatives – provide easy meat for the 'axe'!

Most retailers in fact have a natural leaning towards achieving high standards through the 'hard skills' involved in customer service – these are the factors which noticeably affect customers' willingness to return to your business for reliable quality, price, stock assortment and availability. Get these things wrong, and the effects can be disastrous.

However, it is easy for a business to find itself in a downward spiral of decline, unless the necessary investment of time, money and effort are put into the very functions which can be measured by customers themselves. To a great extent, the customer is the ultimate 'Manager' of the business!

Where 'customer care' initiatives have been applied, they have sometimes consisted of a few hours' training across-the-board, with inadequate attention being given to measuring its effect, individual coaching or follow-up support. The inevitable consequence which staff (and managers) draw from these superficial approaches is simply that 'the box has been ticked' and everything will settle back to normal after the 'day out'. *This book does not recommend this approach, either!*

We have only to see how major UK companies such as British Airways have created a real renaissance in revenue and profit growth – mostly on the back of excellent customer service. It really does work! *But:*

Achieving, and maintaining customer excellence takes a great deal of consistent effort!

3. Levels of experience and development

Customer service, then, is a topic which everyone knows something about. We have all had good experiences, and have laughed at some of the training videos illustrating what not to do!

However, the topic reveals hidden depths as we re-examine it from different perspectives; it is not just about insisting that all staff greet customers with a smile! Instead, it cannot be divorced from:

- the quality and availability of the products or services offered
- the adequacy and 'user friendliness' of the firm's systems which are visible to the customer
- the consistency of implementation of the firm's marketing policy.
- the application of a flexible service style to fit the needs of the firm's customers.

Readers will inevitably have their own enthusiasms and prejudices for the topics included in each chapter of the book. However, it is hoped that, in an attempt to include something for everybody the whole book does not create resistance to a single idea because one element has proved difficult to apply in the past! There will be problems in making the necessary changes to make a lasting improvement in this area. However, consistent efforts by the whole management team will create the right opportunities – given the will to do so. We hope that the book will help generate this will.

4. Looking ahead

The book is presented in three parts:

Part 1 – Managing People – introduces the approaches which make the difference in effectively leading the sales team and concentrates on the good practices used by successful managers.

Part 2 – Managing Customer Service – develops the themes involved in the technical aspects of customer care and how managers should lead new initiatives.

Part 3 – Managing Retail Operations – offers an overview of some of the key management skills which have proved to be of importance in helping to achieve lasting change in operational performance of front-line teams.

Each of these sections contains chapters which seek to guide the reader through the main challenges involved in running a retail business at the 'sharp end'. The book does not displace the need for practical management training but provides a valuable reference point for both new and experienced sales managers.

5. Chapter overviews

Part 1 will be especially helpful to the newly appointed manager who needs guidance on the fundamentals of managing people. From consideration of making the transition (mental and practical) into the new role, Chapter 2 considers the fundamentals of leadership and teamwork. This is followed by the importance of recruiting the best team members that can be afforded under the budget (Chapter 3) leading to an analysis of methods of improving performance (Chapter 4). The section concludes with a review of group communications (Chapter 5) – which so often seem difficult to maintain (with part-timers, shift-workers and, probably, 7-day trading!).

Part 2 covers the modern-day challenges of managing customer service – and this may be of greater interest to the sales manager who has already made the early transition to the new role. Focusing on the desired business culture (Chapter 6), the section provides definitions and illustrations of the customer care challenge (Chapter 7), which will be valuable as the marketplace increases in competition, and promotes some new thinking on the relationship between organisation (chapter 8) and the importance of stimulating a sense of mission (chapter 9) in customer service teams.

Part 3 completes the guide with a review of some of the key issues involved in operating retail businesses – from products and services (Chapter 10) through stock and money management (Chapters 11 and 12) and concluding with a reminder of the issues involved in health and safety (Chapter 13). All these factors make a major contribution to successful retail sales management. However, research shows that successful companies:

- identify with their customer base

- really listen to what their customers have to say
- think as they do
- anticipate their needs
- solve their problems, reliably

… and do all these things profitably! While their customers:

- understand the benefits of dealing with the company
- understand the benefits of using their products/services
- have confidence in the company's business values.

Retailing, or to be more precise, retail management, is a fascinating profession in which it is possible to witness direct results from the implementation of actions and policies.

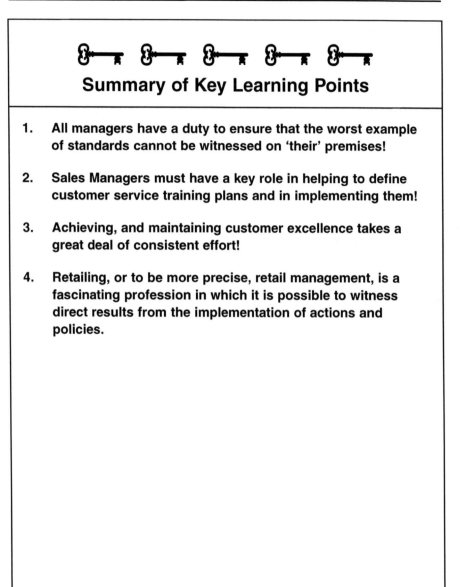

Summary of Key Learning Points

1. **All managers have a duty to ensure that the worst example of standards cannot be witnessed on 'their' premises!**

2. **Sales Managers must have a key role in helping to define customer service training plans and in implementing them!**

3. **Achieving, and maintaining customer excellence takes a great deal of consistent effort!**

4. **Retailing, or to be more precise, retail management, is a fascinating profession in which it is possible to witness direct results from the implementation of actions and policies.**

PART ONE:

MANAGING PEOPLE

'Leaders must be seen to be up front, up-to-date, up to their job and up early in the morning.'

Lord Sieff – former chairman of Marks & Spencer

2

Transition – Teams and Leaders

Advice for the new manager

1. Introduction

'So, now you are the Manager' – it has a good sound to it, doesn't it? You must have worked hard to reach this point – all those extra hours staying late to help clear up when everyone else made for home as quickly as possible, the additional training you attended in your own time, all the effort you made to help newcomers learn about the business and become valuable team members... All this, when you were never really expected to do any of these things as part of your job! So, with any luck, all this will stop now, as you are the manager and you can see that someone else does these things? *Wrong thinking!*

Here is an important message:

> You must have shown already that you are a responsible person – someone who can be trusted with the resources of the business – or you would not have been offered the manager's job. But think back to others you have worked for/with! Did they delegate everything to everyone else and have an "easy" time? Did the team grumble about the managers behind their backs because they wanted the job but never seemed to contribute much themselves – we hope not (but it does happen!). So, would you rather be known as a "supportive manager" – someone who helps the team achieve – rather than someone who imposes jobs on others and fails to show any appreciation of the work of others?
>
> The answer should be obvious!

Now that the job is yours, you'll have the freedom to put all your own ideas into practice, won't you? Some of the things that have frustrated you in the past, when your manager did not quite achieve the result the business was seeking – and you could see a better way but felt he or she might not listen? Well there are some nasty little traps here too! You might find that it isn't quite so easy as you had imagined. And what will happen if the ideas don't work – won't you have lost face and credibility with your staff when it all has to be put into reverse?

These might all seem to be obvious challenges – but they do worry many newly appointed managers and supervisors – 'What will happen if it all goes wrong?'

This book is dedicated to helping you ensure that this does not happen. It is intended to be a practical look at the role of the manager in achieving the very things the firm is seeking – outstanding results! – and it should be as beneficial for the new manager as those who may benefit from a little 'brush-up'!

The advice we have drawn together is taken from a whole range of sources – but mostly from listening to, and advising, thousands of newly appointed managers who have received initial training and counselling through our training workshops. The best sources for successful techniques are successful managers but, unfortunately, they are not always accessible and some do not make the best teachers.

If you are fortunate in having the support of a good coach, then, you will probably want to provide the same support for new and potential managers when it comes to be their 'turn'.

2. The 'honeymoon' period

When career decisions are taken about promotions there is often some uncertainty among those involved as to whether the correct choice has been made. This is very rarely communicated direct to the individuals concerned – only that the organisation is 'pleased to announce that the appointment has been made;' and good luck offered to the new appointee! Behind the scenes, however, some doubts often remain as to whether the new person will be able to succeed with the post, and what help he or she might need.

This sometimes explains the 'honeymoon' period – when the boss is especially supportive with time and advice, and may even provide coaching opportunities when required (and sometimes when not, as well!). You see, the fact is that *the company wants you to succeed!* This may be reflected in closer supervision than you would prefer – or telling you things in fine detail (which you thought were obvious anyway!) – but it is all probably well-intentioned!

It may also be that you work for a highly organised business which provides pre-appointment training – in which case you may have been 'straining at the leash' for some time! This can bring dangers, too.

Over-confidence can sometimes rebound on us at a later date!

If you feel stifled by too much attention from your manager – ask yourself if you would prefer to be 'thrown in at the deep end'? This can prove exceptionally stressful!

What happens when the 'honeymoon' period wears off, then? For some this may be just a week or so after appointment; for most it will be at least a month or two. Will it be back to reality then? Probably!

So how did you see your new boss before you were appointed? Distant? Frightening? Or just very good at motivating people and creating results? You both have some adjustments to make – as with every new relationship – and the strengths and weaknesses of both of you will need to be recognised and compensated for.

For example: Some middle managers are extremely good communicators and leaders – but not awfully good at the paper administration; you may need to compensate for this by becoming better at those aspects yourself.

Case Study: The assistant manager

Clary Smith was the Assistant Manager of Eastern Furnishings – a specialist retail multiple selling exclusive home furnishing fabrics. Her role as Assistant Manager was the day-to-day supervision of her Manager's branch – at which she excelled. The Branch Manager had a reputation in the firm as a good leader (with some charisma!) and something of a sales trainer and the branch was always up on its

Case Study: The assistant manager (cont)

budget. However, he gave rather lower priority to his paperwork – preferring to spend his time on supporting the sales effort by coaching the sales team. Working relationships with Clary were good and he was always very appreciative of her efforts as the senior sales person of the team.

From the Regional Manager's viewpoint, the branch could always be counted on for a positive response to anything new – policies, stock ranges etc. He was prepared to overlook the occasional "blip" with the administration (he had been a successful Sales Manager himself, and got away with minimal time spent on administration!).

In the New Year promotions, the Branch Manager was promoted to regional Manager in another area and his position was offered to Clary. She was exceptionally flattered to have the offer, but said to the boss that she would need some training on her administration responsibilities. He agreed – and offered to spend some time with her – but also expressed some surprise that she should feel the need for any help as her Manager had such a good reputation as a trainer/coach.

Clary's first few weeks in the new job were exceptionally busy, with the 4-week Winter Sale; and the Regional Manager visited her briefly in the first week, but otherwise left her alone! By the time she got round to sorting out all the invoices, credits, stock records etc there was nearly a two months' backlog. She telephoned the Regional Manager's office for advice – to discover he had been sent on a management development programme in France and he would not be back for another 4 weeks. Then the telephone call came from the Head of Accounts. In short, he threatened that, if her accounts were not cleared within 24 hours, he would report her to the Board.

After a sleepless night, Clary posted a letter of resignation and phoned in sick.

Points for consideration:

a) Who was to blame for this situation?

b) What should have happened?

c) How could this be avoided in the future?

Discuss your views of this incident with your manager. Could it happen at your firm?

3. The manager's task

Up until now you have only had to look after yourself at work. Now that you are the manager, you will have to come to terms with one fundamental change:

Your needs are less important than those of your team!

You might have noticed from observing other managers (including your last one) that, when things go badly, the pressure (or even 'blame'), more often than not, is directed at the manager. But, when things go well, the praise is attributed to his or her team! Why is this?

The fact is that a good manager will not expect anything else. Your satisfaction should be gained, not from 'basking in the sunshine of praise from your boss', but from the sense of achievement through your team's success and the feeling that they will continue to grow in ability (providing opportunities to continue to improve results over a period of time).

In other words, the credit for good performance should go to the whole team – rather than to you – and, if this works well, you will find that you have a stronger and more motivated team which will be seeking the increased results that you have been set!

So, what is the manager's task? You may have been given a list of responsibilities (or a job description) with your letter of appointment and this should provide a useful checklist of duties. However, what it may not convey is the 'big picture'.

Many writers have attempted to describe the function of the manager and it is worth quoting two of them. Peter Drucker, one of the earliest management 'gurus', describes the manager's function as:

A manager is a person who achieves performance objectives through the best use of the 5 key resources – Money, People, Equipment, Materials (Stock), and Time!

Does this sound simple? Ask yourself what are your responsibilities and performance objectives? The following assignment may help to answer the question:

Assignment: Resource management

What are your responsibilities under those 5 resource areas Peter Drucker listed?

a) Money (e.g. security, banking, etc.)

____

____

____

b) People (e.g. recruiting, training, discipline, etc.)

____

____

____

c) Equipment/Fixturing/Premises (e.g. maintenance, usage, etc.)

d) Stock (materials) (e.g. stockholding value, stock-turn, mark-downs, etc.)

e) Time (e.g. best uses of time, own and others' timekeeping, etc.)

This kind of checklist should provide you with a valuable overview of the role which you are expected to fill – if you have any doubts about whether the picture is complete, you should check it out with your manager.

Of course, this is only one part of the picture. Another essential aspect is the outputs from your job – the ways in which your contribution will be measured. To gain a clearer picture of these outputs, you should take another look at each item above and add those performance measures alongside.

For example, an output from managing people well could be reflected in low staff turnover figures and in the value of sales-per-employee you are achieving. (These might include measurable results as well as [illegible] objective factors; you might need to consult your new manager to be [illegible] complete this assignment).

When you have completed this assignment, it woul[illegible] how you see the job, with your boss – have you mi[illegible] included something which is really someone else's [illegible]

4. The 'new manager' in context

With a clearer perspective on your resource responsibilities and how your performance will be judged, we can now look at some of the methods of achieving the results.

John Adair, another leading management author, identified the importance of managers becoming leaders. There is an important distinction here:

A leader has a vital role in developing a team and encouraging all members to work together as effective members of that team.

He developed the following 'model':

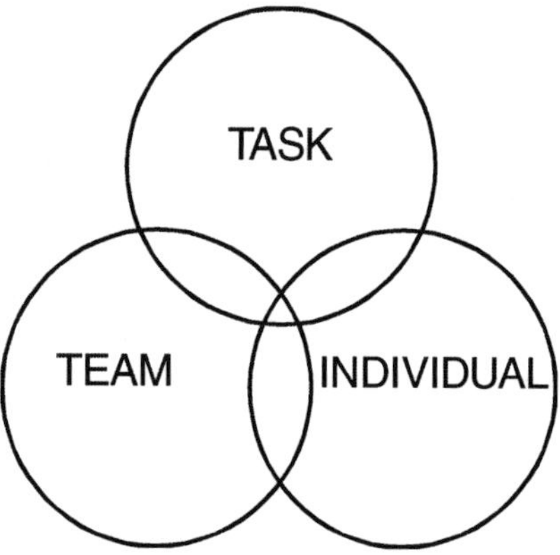

The whole point of this diagram is that it shows the relationship between the three areas of responsibility. If any one of the three circles is 'eclipsed' (or performance in that area is poor), then there will be a detrimental effect on the other two. So, for example, where the task is not being achieved, (e.g. sales are not up to target), the team may feel demotivated and one or two individuals may even consider 'jumping ship' before things get too bad! By reverse argument:

When everything is going well, all three 'zones' will be working well and a highly motivated and successful team should result!

5. The task

The earlier sections have identified the importance of creating good results; the team may look to the boss to be more than a successful business-person.

Actual sales, profit margins, stockturn, mark-downs, losses, all need to beat (or at least match) the targets set by the business but the human factors need to be considered as well!

... as we shall see in the next section. However, future financial security and success in the business result directly from task achievement. This means the manager needs to have a thorough understanding of the technical aspects of retailing listed above.

6. Individual needs

Your team is made up of a number of individuals – each one with different hopes, fears, needs and aspirations. You will probably remember all too vividly what it felt like when you were made to feel 'just a number' – or even a 'till stuffer' – by a past manager. We all tend to work much better when our individuality is respected and we feel valued as a person. However, a manager's time is precious and there is a limit to the amount of time any of us can dedicate to individuals – and still get the work done! The bigger the team, the larger this particular challenge is – and it has been said that the maximum number of people one manager can successfully lead (without the assistance of a deputy or supervisor) is 8-11. Even when work teams have gone through the process known as 'empowerment', individuals still need positive encouragement from the boss - and access so that personal support is possible.

What sort of support do people expect from their boss? A recent survey showed that the following activities are highly valued by team members:

- one-to-one coaching and instruction
- praise and encouragement
- appraisal and reviews of performance
- listening, counselling and helping to solve problems
- discipline – when necessary.

The biggest challenge in meeting these expectations is probably finding the time for them – but this does not diminish their importance! The extraordinary fact is that the most amount of time a manager may spend with a team member (on their own) is probably right at the start of the relationship – when they are first interviewed and selected. After that, the really important activities, such as coaching support, are needed. The quality of the manager's response will have a large effect on the degree of effort and motivation the staff member puts into their job during what they may see as the daily grind of earning a living. You can help them see that their job is much broader than that!

The individual needs to have the following briefing, at least, responding to the individual's expectations:

- 'tell me what you expect of me' (do you have a list of duties for me?)
- 'tell me how you want it done' (can I have an induction briefing?)
- 'let me know what progress I am making' (a balanced appraisal or assessment meeting would be a fair way)
- 'reward me in proportion to my effort and results'
- 'give me help/advice on how to develop my skills as I need it' (please give me some training!)

If this all seems like common sense, can you put your hand on your heart and say that you have supplied this support for all your team? (Everything may not be your own task – but have you tried to ensure that the task has been undertaken by someone?).

7. Group needs

Everyone (except a real 'loner') needs to build good relationships with their work colleagues; and this is not always the easiest factor to achieve inside a team. Petty jealousies, irritations and upsets can quickly create animosity and bad feelings in a team – and it generally falls to the manager to keep these factors under control. It has been argued that the manager or leader should provide the vision or 'sticking plaster' which creates the wish for team members to unite and pull together. Anyone who has worked in a team in which constant bickering and upsets have featured, will know that the manager's influence is vital in bringing the best out of team members – it is sometimes known as 'putting the interests of the team before those of the individual' (and various sporting captains have been seen to be juggling with these demands as particular players have variously come into, and fallen out of, form!).

What makes people want to work successfully as team members?

Most importantly, it is the feeling that they belong to a *'winning team'!* The quality of success may elude some managers – and it certainly is not a pre-requisite for the manager or leader to be liked by every team member (or vice versa). However, success breeds respect – for the leader who proves his or her skill in taking the right (and timely) decisions; and respect is a two-way street.

Case History

An enthusiastic retail trainee had tried to be as helpful as possible for a customer requesting advice about a technical product. In truth, the trainee's knowledge was inadequate; and the more he tried to help, so it became increasingly obvious to the customer that he did not know what he was talking about. The customer lost all respect for the firm and left the department, lodging a complaint with the Sales Manager on the way out!

This angered the Manager, so he then immediately tore a strip off the trainee – instructing him not to make up answers, but always to ask for help! This whole, heated conversation took place on the shop floor – in front of other sales staff and customers.

How do you feel about this example?

Clearly, a real training need existed here – for both individuals. The trainee needed to improve his product knowledge quickly – and the manager needed to learn how to deal with situations like that. There was nothing wrong with addressing the mis-description of goods issue. However, it should have been dealt with off-the-job, in the office and out of earshot of other people! What respect would the team have for the manager after this outburst?

8. Challenging situations

The 'Star'

'Star' performers have been known to hold their managers (and the rest of the team) 'to ransom' – perhaps by 'working to rule' – not trying hard enough, going sick, etc. If they really are star performers and results take a 'nose-dive' when they are away, you could have a real difficulty. The time may come when there is a 'trial of strength' between you, and you may feel you have to back down for fear of losing them altogether. There is a medium/long term solution to this – but one which may sound harder than it really is.

Quite often, team members feel a small sense of resentment when they are in the 'shadow' of an individual who is so much better a performer than themselves. It is easy to see why – often the 'star' turn is mentioned in company newsletters, is offered more training than the rest, is allowed to have holidays/days off just when they like. It is understood why all this happens – but not approved of!

Without explicitly overturning these customs, the manager's task is to ensure a fair balance between all team members – and the best insurance policy for this would be to ensure that all team members have similar training opportunities – and rewards – as they increase their competence and performance! The 'star' will quickly come to recognise the importance of this policy to the whole team and may even be prepared to take a hand in the training (a sense of loyalty to the team should make him or her want the team to be successful – especially if he or she has ambitions to become a manager, too!).

How do you find out these things? Simple. You ask!

As we will see in the next chapter, the manager has relationships with the team as a whole – and with the individuals that make it up.

The secret of successful transition is to maintain each level of team relationships in balance – together with the good relationship with the boss!

The non-promoted 'front-runner'

Were you appointed to your position over the head of another team member? No matter how hard we try not to convince ourselves that promotion is ours, most people are likely to feel some disappointment – and even some resentment – that they were not chosen. It is important to remember that 'being passed over' is not a judgement about a person's capability to do the present job – only that it has been thought that the qualities and skills needed in the new manager are stronger in the appointee. If you are the new manager, you may need to point this out to any staff member who may feel hurt by your appointment.

The best way to do this is in a private 'one-to-one' meeting in which your aims should be to provide:

- reassurance that the person is valued
- explanation of your views and goals for the team in the future
- seeking their continued support for the team and you as leader
- recognition of their important role in promoting strong team performance.

It is amazing how well this approach works.

Few people really want to put the team's reputation and performance in jeopardy, even when they are feeling personally sore that they missed out on the leader's job!

Shortage of team members

Another challenge which can occur – especially if trade is poor or shaky – is when, with your promotion, your new boss withholds his authority to recruit a replacement for you.

If your promotion was from within the department, the lack of a replacement will probably mean that your team will have to work one person short. There may be a reasonable argument for this but it may not be appreciated by the rest of the team – who may feel they will be expected to work even harder than previously. If you are unable to convince them of the logic of this personnel decision, you may experience a lowering of team morale (this can also have a negative effect on the team's enthusiasm for achieving the set targets). There is no easy solution to this; the new manager will need to assemble the facts of the case:

- how many team members have been employed in past years (not just the immediate past)
- sales records could then be divided by the total team numbers (if several part-timers are employed, this may need to be calculated on the basis of 'full-time equivalents')

- the resulting sales-per-person employed can then be compared with the current results and this may reveal whether a replacement person could be afforded.

(Obviously, if these calculations do not prove the point, you may have to drop your case and present the reasons for not recruiting to convince your team!)

9. Perspectives of success

Many recipes for success in management have been promoted by experienced managers, authors and trainers. What many forget to mention is that success may be measured in several dimensions and by different people:

- as measured by senior management
- historical comparison
- as measured by the team
- as measured by customers.

Surely, you might think, all these perspectives should be rolled into one? Often, however, it seems that one dimension is viewed as more important than the rest. In this section, we will set out some of the secrets of success – as used by successful managers – and explore some of the 'traps' which can open up in front of us – which may prevent that constant drive for good results!

Targets and objectives

As we saw in the previous chapter, every manager should have a clear understanding about how performance is to be measured by the organisation and the boss; it makes no sense to be propelling an unguided 'rocket' into space... Management is a complicated enough task without the additional complication of having no targets to shoot at!

In retailing, it has to be said that setting measurable targets for managers is rarely a problem. Because the industry is business oriented, departmental targets are normally expressed in terms of sales to be achieved (and probably Gross Profit or Margin) – but how many?

Beating last year's sales figures may not be good enough without some allowance for price inflation (or we may just be standing still); and then there is the thought about the business growing. Even in periods when the total market for your firm's products or services is static, the firm may still have expectations of growth – against the performance of other businesses in the area. In other words – to increase the share of the available business and penetrate the market more successfully. So, a target of 7.5% increase over a previous year may not look quite so unrealistic when it includes an allowance for price inflation of around 2.5%.

Few retailers are satisfied with setting targets which are geared only to sales. Sales figures are simply a means to a most important end – making a profit. Managers should make a significant contribution to doing this in their branches, departments, and for the business as a whole. But *profit has to be the primary objective.*

Profits can be lost through a poorly organised and run business – a drain in profits may be accounted for by:

- cash shortages and errors
- mark-downs
- stock losses – through breakages or even theft
- failure to rotate stock and sell old stock first
- lack of control of overheads and expenses.

The new manager should be thoroughly briefed on the firm's expectations – but, sadly, this is not always done thoroughly, leading to possible misunderstandings and disappointments. Imagine the scene of a performance review in which the manager is expecting a 'gold star' for outstanding sales achievements only to discover that there is a risk that the branch might even be closed down as its profit contribution is so poor.

Sound manager performance can be defeated through poor or incomplete briefing. If good briefing is absent, it is essential that the manager requests the vital information!

Assignment: Measures of success

Write a list of the criteria which will be used in measuring your performance in your job. Express them as objectives or goals.

If you find this difficult to do – or you are unsure in any way, please ask your manager to explain them to you.

Objectives/goals

1 ______________________________

2 ______________________________

3 ______________________________

4 ______________________________

One of the most important marks of outstanding managers is their focus on the team's results – and their constant pursuit of ways of improving them. This does not mean forcing everyone to monitor their own performance minute-by-minute and living in a perpetual state of misery when expectations are not being met! However, it does mean keeping an 'eye on the ball' all the time – and encouraging others to do the same. So, the above chart ought to have two more columns added – a comparison column in which actuals may be compared with the target, and an action plan column which encourages the devising and noting of action which can be taken either to exploit success or overcome a shortfall.

Objectives/goals	Actuals	Action Plans
1		
2		
3		
4		
5		

And, by the way, what is the point of having this written down? 'Why can't we just carry it in our heads' – many managers have been heard to say – 'We have more than enough paperwork already!'

Tracking sales and profits is a crucial function of managers – at all levels of a retail business!

... and the kind of table offered above helps to focus the local manager's attention to two tasks:

- what action to take to correct performance – where it has failed to match the targets
- how the team can be encouraged to exploit good performance – and gain an even greater contribution to the 'bottom line'.

This does not guarantee that Senior Managers will be more tolerant of a manager and team who keep missing their targets, but they will be slightly more understanding if they feel that the manager is constantly looking for ways to 'stir up the local market' and gain more business (we will return to this theme in Chapter 5 – Brainstorming).

Case History

Flannels, a high fashion retailer based in the North West of England, has a strong reputation for sales and service – especially in designer clothing. Considerable emphasis is placed on the role of the branch and departmental managers – many of whom are under the age of 30/25.

A recent leadership workshop highlighted the need for teamworking, enthusiastic management and the importance of maximising customer service and selling skills. All participants produced personal action plans to guide post-course application and their senior managers reported an improvement in service standards as a result.

A typical report from one branch manager read: "The workshop helped me recognise that the challenges I faced were shared by other managers in the group – I was not alone! The training gave me the confidence to take positive action in improving selling skills and the standards of the team. Branch results have certainly improved as a consequence".

Challenges and 'traps'

As we have seen there are many traps which seem to be placed in the way of managers. Some may be of their own making – others may arise from the specific circumstances of the business. The two categories are:

- 'Letting-go' of the old job
- Self-imposed challenges.

'Letting-go' of the old job

We have already seen that good leaders do not set themselves up as if they are in competition with members of their own teams; the manager should not aim to be the best 'striker', 'defender', 'goal-keeper', 'throw-in' or 'corner-taker'! But this is very tempting – especially if the manager finds it difficult to adapt to the new role.

It is part of the natural temperament of many people that, in the face of difficulties or lack of understanding in the job, that they should concentrate on the parts of the job which they most enjoy – and these tend to be those tasks in which they are highly skilled. It follows then that, rather than concentrating on supporting and coaching team members, the new manager may fall into the 'trap' of competing with them.

This does not mean that the manager should never help the sales effort (or take part in some of the other team duties), but there should always be a secondary motive involved. In other words, contributing to the sales effort will be a more effective use of the manager's time if it is offered as:

- a standard-setting example for a new team member
- relief for a staff member who is in need of a break
- coaching for a sales person who is finding a particular customer difficult to 'close'.

Other non-selling duties, for example making the coffee or sweeping-up, might be undertaken as an element of leadership (demonstrating that the manager is not above doing these things) – but certainly not as a matter of routine.

There is almost certainly a differential between the manager's salary and that of the rest of the team; the firm is receiving poor value for money if the manager insists on carrying out tasks which should be undertaken by team members!

Self-imposed challenges

Some managers find themselves tempted to 'tilt at windmills' – determined to build a personal reputation for some of the following examples:

- efficiency in all paperwork
- best stockturn in the company
- lowest complaints record
- most creative displays.

Obviously, all these factors are important contributors to the overall targets set for the team to achieve. However, over-concentration on any single item can quickly become an obsession and cause the manager to lose a sense of balance in the operation of the branch or department. This is also likely to be monitored in any performance reviews carried out by the manager's manager – with the aim of encouraging the job holder to be a 'fully rounded' manager – capable of performing with equal strength across the full range of retail functions required in the job.

10. Summary

This chapter has sought to set the scene on the critical role which is fulfilled by department and branch managers. The job can be, at the same time, both a fascinating challenge and an irritating frustration – especially when the market fails to respond to the efforts which are being made by the sales team. However, with consistent quality of work and excellent customer service, managers may have to look for other reasons (some which may be beyond their control) for a poor market reaction.

Following chapters will also serve as a valuable checklist to help identify positive action points which the manager can take in pursuit of better performance.

Summary of Key Learning Points

1. The best sources for successful techniques are successful managers but, unfortunately, they are not always accessible and some do not make the best teachers.

2. Over-confidence can sometimes rebound on us at a later date.

3. Your needs are less important than those of your team.

4. Are you a person who achieves performance objectives through the best use of the 5 key resources – Money, People, Equipment, Materials (Stock), and Time?

5. A leader has a vital role in developing a team and encouraging all members to work together as effective members of that team.

6. Actual sales, profit margins, stockturn, mark-downs, losses, all need to beat (or at least match) the targets set by the business but the human factors need to be considered as well .

7. When everything is going well, all three 'zones'(Task, Team, Individual) will be working well and a highly motivated and successful team should result.

8. The secret of successful transition is to maintain each level of team relationships in balance – together with the relationship with the boss!

9. Few people really want to put the team's reputation and performance into jeopardy, even when they are feeling

Summary of Key Learning Points

personally sore that they missed out on the leader's job.

10. Sound manager performance can be defeated through poor or incomplete briefing. If good briefing is absent, it is essential that the manager requests the vital information.

11. Tracking sales and profits is a crucial function of managers – at all levels of a retail business .

12. There is almost certainly a salary differential between the manager's salary and that of the rest of the team; the firm is receiving poor value for money if the manager habitually carries out tasks which should be undertaken by team members.

3

Get Good People First!

They are easier to train and they perform better

1. Introduction

For as long as I can remember, businesses have complained that they have been unable to obtain either sufficient staff – or people of the best quality – or both! However, if this were entirely true, then sales targets would not be met, and many more businesses would have collapsed and closed down than happened through two major recessions (in the 1980's and 90's). The truth is that we can always imagine how good it would be if all our existing staff were perfect and every new applicant was a self-starter (with all the skills matching the best of your experienced staff), but reality is different. The fact is that, unless we are exceptionally lucky, we will nearly always have to take on less experienced (and possibly untrained people) and then set about training them.

Experienced managers know that, much as we might like to think otherwise, people are a moving resource in the business – not just changing in numbers (joiners and leavers) but also changing in terms of quality and performance. Chapter 4 will explore this in more depth – but:

The whole process of managing people's performance (and training them) is made much easier if you get good people first!

This is the main theme of this chapter – how to attract and appoint the most suitable people to your vacancies. We will consider:

- the importance of setting high standards in recruitment
- the need to define the roles which need to be filled
- identifying the essential and desirable qualities of applicants

- attracting the right level of applicants
- managing the selection process
- making the appointment.

Throughout this chapter, we will emphasise the need for a 'seamless' recruitment and selection process. Even if the reader is not personally responsible for 'hiring' and 'firing' staff, you are responsible for helping them achieve results, and therefore it is down to you to influence the processes whereby new staff are recruited. This may involve time spent with your Company's Personnel Officer or Managing Director – Employment Agencies, or Careers Officers. Such time will not be wasted if you have already undertaken the steps described in this chapter.

2. Setting high standards in recruitment

Managers with a 'siege mentality' may be tempted to fill vacancies by taking the first people who present themselves, regardless of their qualities, skills, personality or general attributes!

This is the policy of desperation and may lead to diluting what standards the business currently has. If no standards are set, it should not be surprising if none are attained!

This argument is not dependent on the wages or salaries that the business is able to offer – although this will have a bearing on the level of applications which the organisation may attract. 'Pay peanuts and you are likely to attract monkeys' is the rather unkind adage. Unkind? Yes, but some applicants may be happy to trade their hourly rate just to get back into employment – the question is, will they settle in the business and still be as enthusiastic in 12 or 18 months time? Others may see your position as a 'stepping stone' towards something better in due course – perhaps a trade-off between wages and training offered and longer term career prospects. The whole process of recruitment can usefully be tackled from the marketing standpoint.

So what kinds of standards might be set? A pleasing personality and interest in (and willingness to help) people could be viewed as essential – but also some indication of achievements as well. Some positions may require reasonable arithmetical skills (e.g. in estimating or measuring and fitting) or the ability to write persuasive letters to customers. Even if these skills are not required for a year or two, it could be a terrible disadvantage if you suddenly discover that your 'star' employee cannot write or do multiplication sums!

Achieving a better quality of recruits in a business depends to a large extent on your attitude of mind!

The days of queues of potential candidates forming outside your business may have long gone but some employers have built up good reputations for providing interesting work, adequate training and satisfactory remuneration and they are the ones who never seem to have any difficulty in recruiting good people. So, employment reputations can operate like a spiral – get everything right and the reputation goes up, get it wrong and it can be progressively more difficult to attract high-fliers. (In today's increasingly competitive market place, employers have the opportunity to achieve some external accreditation for their employment processes – for example the 'Investors in People' award which provides a useful seal of approval and a way of promoting the business to the community).

This whole process should not be confused with levels of qualifications. It is not necessary for most entrants into a retail selling career to have a degree in Biology – or even Business Studies – although this level of academic achievement may be an excellent indication of the individual's ability to perform to this high standard (which may be a good indicator of potential to take on more responsibility later on).

Similarly, achievement of some General National Vocational Qualifications (GNVQs) at school may help establish a baseline for school-leavers – but even these may be less important than the ability to present themselves confidently with some forethought about their personal appearance and impact.

The truth is that qualifications alone do not necessarily provide a guarantee of performance – and the job may not demand them anyway, as we shall see next.

3. Define the role

What kinds of responsibilities do you wish your new employee(s) to carry? The answer – 'to sell our products' – is both obvious and yet oversimplified.

Retailing in quality businesses involves a great deal more than 'standing in the shop taking money and wrapping goods' but the full story is often overlooked in recruitment advertisements and literature!

The most important quality that new staff need is 'customer awareness' – the ability to want to put customers first and provide them with the best quality care and service that they can. Some of this enthusiasm or motivation may be latent inside the applicant, but it also needs to be brought out as the staff member fits into the new role – and is trained to meet the performance standards of the business.

What kinds of standards might be set? This topic is covered in more detail in Chapter 7 – suffice to say here that a business could adopt the following kinds of performance standards at the 'front end' of the business:

- to greet all visitors into the stores within 30 seconds of their arrival
- to put customers first by dropping any other task and focusing on their needs promptly
- to be a 'team player' by accepting 'non-selling duties' as well as customer care tasks
- to maintain up-to-date product knowledge so that they can advise customers on their purchases
- to be able to close sales and introduce related purchase opportunities whenever possible.

How does this abbreviated list compare with your understanding of task needs in your business? If you are about to recruit a new sales-person shortly, you will find the following assignment valuable:

Assignment

On the following chart, list the responsibilities you will expect your new employee to fill:

Customers ____

____

____

Stock ____

____

____

Money/Transactions/Systems ____

____

____

Maintenance/Stock-keeping/Cleaning ____

____

____

Now would be a good moment to consider the ways in which you will be able to measure the success of the individual in this role - and add these measures to your list of tasks/responsibilities (on the chart opposite). For example, under the Customers section it might be prudent to identify the salesperson's conversion rate (i.e. how many visitors have been 'converted' into customers); in the Money/Transactions/Systems category measures would include a cash register which balances every day.

4. Draft a 'person profile'

In today's highly competitive retail market, personnel have become an important marketing 'weapon' in firms' bids to maximise their market share and achieve growing sales performance!

Responsibilities/Tasks	**Measures of performance**
Customers	
______________________________	______________________________
______________________________	______________________________
______________________________	______________________________
Stock	
______________________________	______________________________
______________________________	______________________________
______________________________	______________________________
Money/Transactions/Systems	
______________________________	______________________________
______________________________	______________________________
______________________________	______________________________
Maintenance/Stock-keeping/Cleaning	
______________________________	______________________________
______________________________	______________________________
______________________________	______________________________

It is true that, in reactive/quick service sectors of retailing, customers may simply need efficient, speedy service – preferably with a smile! However, in so many other sectors and departments (especially those where customers' purchasing decisions are influenced by product information and sales techniques – mostly in high value sales) intelligent and skilled sales staff can make all the difference between average and outstanding sales performance.

In our earlier book, '*Retail Selling*', we contrasted prime differences between order-takers and professional sellers and the following example illustrates how these might be reflected in the recruitment process by using a 'person profile'.

A person profile is an 'Identikit' picture of the person who you believe will be most successful in the job. In larger firms this picture may be drafted by the Personnel specialists in the business. However, it is important for the

l comment on the standards that may have been drafted
:tion's behalf. This profile is a crucial document which
e recruitment standards which the firm aspires to (see

ould be a wonderful world if it were easy to obtain staff who match all the standards which are described in the person profile. Sadly, this is less likely to happen in reality so it is essential to build some flexibility into the standards and so distinguish between acceptable standards and ideal standards.

Care should be taken here not to fix on any subjective standards which might be taken as discriminatory on grounds of sex, race, age, religion, or disability which, if practised, may be illegal!

Here is a completed example for the first section of a typical person profile for a salesperson.

Factor	Essential	Desirable
Greets visitors promptly	Warm, outgoing nature	Bubbly personality
Puts customers' needs first	Responsible sense of priorities	Thinks things through
Accepts 'Team Player' role	Prepared to undertake all types of tasks	Volunteers for additional tasks/ responsibilities
Keeps product knowledge up-to-date	Evidence of practical interest in your stocks	Actively seeks out new product information

5. Attracting the right level of applicants

In just the same way as the business tries to attract customers, managers are frequently confronted with the need to market a vacancy to the public. There are a multitude of methods which may be used – from the least expensive (for example, a vacancy card posted in the retailer's front window) to the most expensive (for example, advertising in a daily newspaper) – and each has its strengths and weaknesses. What should be remembered is that:

The process of matching the skills and attributes of applicants to the vacancy requires a reasonable number of applicants from which a selection is possible (although, actually, only one 'perfect-fit' candidate is needed!)

The problem is that, until the applications are received – and, at least some of the most likely candidates are interviewed – the real standard cannot be fairly judged.

In some parts of the UK, one simple newspaper advertisement could attract a very substantial number of applications and it may not be possible to interview everyone. However, it is important that every application is acknowledged – even if they do not proceed to the next stage. You never know who is applying – they may turn out to be regular customers or a local person who can influence lots of other potential customers. If you upset them, you may also lose a lot of local business.

Even if an advertisement is not used, there is always the chance of a high response and this is another good reason for using a major element of 'selection criteria' to exclude a large proportion of candidates.

For example, in a Furnishings business it may be considered *essential* that applicants have had some previous retailing experience but *desirable* that the experience was in a similar business to your own (quality level of trade/degree of customer services offered/product range). The use of the second criteria element may exclude the largest proportion of the applicants – which is fine as long as there is still an adequate mix left in the shortlist from which a choice may still be made. Mistakes can be easily made in 'talking ourselves into' accepting one candidate from the evidence on the application form and become really disappointed by the way in which they interview. A lot of time can be wasted this way.

So, it might be best to plan the process from the output end:

- How many candidates should I short-list? (maybe, 4 good ones?)
- How many should I have on the first interview list? (perhaps 12-14?)
- How many applications, in total, might result in these interviewees? (in some situations, it could be as many as 60!)

It can be readily seen that a simple screening interview of around 30-40 minutes could involve an investment of more than 6 to 7 hours – and this is before we consider the final interview (which ought to be more thorough, and therefore longer).

This may seem obvious, but the best way of helping to screen such a high number of applicants is by using an application form. This will help to ensure that the applicants that are selected for the first 'round' of interviews at least meet the minimum criteria on the person profile.

6. Managing the selection process

Interviewing is a notoriously subjective method of selection but it can still be one of the best if it is controlled properly (and perhaps matched with some more objective methods – such as selection tests).

A good starting point in selection is to prepare a 'battery' of standard questions which should be posed to all the candidates selected for interview!

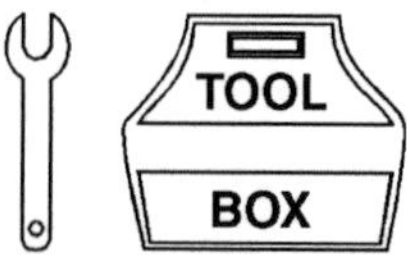

Interview questions

Applicants for a salesperson's position might be asked:

> "What gives you greatest satisfaction in your job as a Sales Assistant?"
>
> "What do you consider are your greatest strengths? And biggest frustrations?"
>
> "A customer finds it difficult to choose between two similar products priced at virtually the same level; how would you close the sale?"

Standard questions like these can provide the basis for comparing the answers of each candidate and, given the way the answers are presented, some further judgements might follow concerning the person's interpersonal skills.

Interviewing a number of candidates can become confusing by the end of the day – and it is important to group them closely together if you are to make valid comparisons.

Some managers ask candidates for a recent photograph – and some firms even take a Polaroid photograph to help the memory.

Another tip is to use a rating form for the interview (see end of chapter). This is particularly helpful if two interviewers are involved – each should complete the rating separately, after each interview, and then compare notes. Any resulting 'disagreements' will reveal just how subjective our ratings can sometimes be!

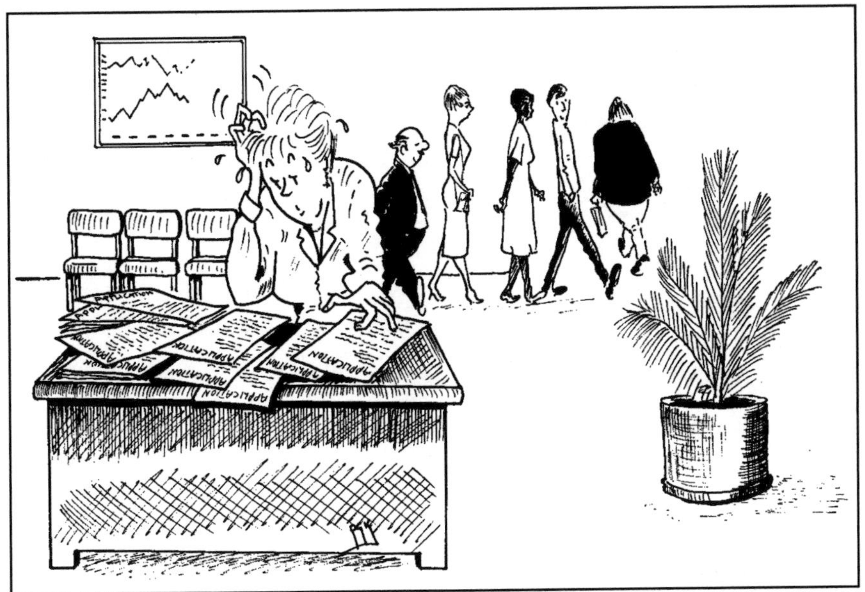

The selection process is likely to be more accurate when the source of evidence that helps the judgement is as wide as possible. Apart from interviewing in pairs or panels, some firms offer candidates the opportunity of a brief guided tour – provided by a senior staff member of their intended team – and any information from the resulting conversation may also be passed to the selection panel.

7. Making the appointment

Obviously job offers form an important part of the employment contract and therefore should be in writing. However, it can protract the process quite a long time if the manager has to wait for letters to be exchanged. Many firms try to speed up the process by making the offer by telephone first.

> *'If we were to make you the offer of the job as we discussed in the interview (confirm the vital details – hours, salary, benefits etc), would you accept?'*

Listen hard at this point for any hesitation – as this could extend into a rejection. A verbal acceptance can then be confirmed in a written offer and acceptance.

If, however, the candidate decides to reject the post, it may be possible/desirable to offer the job to the second best applicant – and no one is any the wiser that they were the second choice. It is important that this process is conducted speedily as, once employees have decided to leave their current jobs, they tend to apply for several new positions at a time. If the process is very delayed, you may find that your best selected candidate has been snapped up by a competitor.

The last stage is to take up references offered. You should always do this – but only look for confirmatory evidence that your selection decision was sound. It has been known to happen that referees have revealed some contra-indication of the person's suitability for the post and that this information had been left out of the interview. In very extreme cases, this could jeopardise the basis of the contract which had been made.

A contract should be made subject to satisfactory references being received – and, even then, many organisations have a probationary period to be served before the employee is confirmed in the position!

Summary

Staff selection is one of the most important tasks a manager is ever asked to do; get it wrong and the consequences may affect the team (and its performance) for quite a long while ahead!

On the other hand, there is no doubt that recruiting his or her own team gives a manager a great bonus start in building the team and creating high performance. It is potentially harder to remould a team which someone else selected – and it may take longer – but care does need to be taken with the selection of a person who will fit in with the established team.

This chapter may have, unintentionally, given the impression that the manager should exercise great caution in recruiting but, as with other tasks, there is room for some risk-taking as well! Selling is easier when sales staff have interesting, lively personalities and one or two 'larger-than-life' characters in a team will help to spice up the team as a whole. However the manager does need to maintain control and, in a responsible, law-abiding business, care needs to be taken to avoid sales staff who may be tempted to be economical with the truth in sales interviews, when making the sale is seen as the most vital aspect of the task!

However, with strong leadership, the manager should aim to bring the best out of the team and still achieve outstanding results. This aspect will be re-addressed in Part 2 of the book.

Summary of Key Learning Points

1. The whole process of managing people's performance (and training them) is made much easier if you get good people first!

2. Achieving a better quality of recruits in a business depends to a large extent on your attitude of mind. Managers with a 'siege mentality' may be tempted to fill vacancies with the first people who present themselves – regardless of their qualities, skills, personality or general attributes.

3. Qualifications alone do not necessarily provide a guarantee of performance – and the job may not demand them anyway.

4. In today's highly competitive retail market, personnel have become an important marketing 'weapon' in firms' bids to maximise their market share and achieve growing sales performance.

5. Retailing in quality businesses involves a great deal more than 'standing in the shop taking money and wrapping goods' but the full story is often overlooked in recruitment advertisements and literature.

6. Care should be taken here not to fix on any subjective standards which might be taken as discriminatory on grounds of sex, race, age, religion, or disability which, if practised, may be illegal.

7. The process of matching the skills and attributes of applicants to the vacancy requires a reasonable number of applicants from which a selection is possible (although, actually, only one 'perfect-fit' candidate is needed!)

Summary of Key Learning Points

8. A good starting point in selection is to prepare a 'battery' of standard questions which should be posed to all the candidates selected for interview.

9. Interviewing a number of candidates can become confusing by the end of the day – and it is important to group them closely together if you are to make valid comparisons.

10. The selection process is likely to be more accurate when the source of evidence that helps the judgement is as wide as possible. Apart from interviewing in pairs or panels, some firms offer candidates the opportunity of a brief guided tour – provided by a senior staff member of their intended team – and any information from the resulting conversation may also be passed to the selection panel.

11. A contract should be made subject to satisfactory references being received – and, even then, many organisations have a probationary period to be served before the employee is confirmed in the position.

12. Staff selection is one of the most important tasks a manager is ever asked to do; get it wrong and the consequences may affect the team (and its performance) for quite a long while ahead.

4

Improving Performance

The 'nuts and bolts' of constant improvement

1. Introduction

If all managers are accountable for the results of their teams, then it would seem to be self-evident that they must also be responsible for improving their performance too. This obvious truth is sadly not always matched in practice. Training and coaching are still functions which are all too often seen by line managers as the province of the central specialist – with the result that the team is left with little practical help at the 'sharp end' of the business.

Why should this be? Often, it reflects poor time management on behalf of the manager – a failure to set priorities, delegate all those items which are not essential for the manager to undertake, and to invest time to achieve that improvement in skills and performance which sometimes seems so elusive! As we saw at the beginning of this book, becoming a good Sales Manager does not happen automatically.

Apart from the fact that you would fail if you tried to do this impossible feat, you would also demotivate all your staff around you too.

So, this chapter considers ways in which managers can achieve improvements in team performance – by balancing their concern for output with concern for people; one should be seen as totally dependent upon the other. Apart from trying to maintain this balancing act there are a number of techniques and systems available to help managers take the right steps in seeking continuous improvement. They are:

- Induction training
- Reviewing (or appraising) performance
- Counselling

- Coaching
- Grievance procedures
- Discipline.

This chapter explores the manager's role in each of these functions.

Moving from a good 'doer' to becoming a good manager of 'doers' initially requires recognition that you can no longer do everything yourself!

2. Induction training

This may seem obvious, but the first challenge that the manager faces after selecting a new team member is to provide adequate induction training for them. Even experienced sales staff will need induction and basic training – especially on your company's ways of doing things (and this means a lot more than just till procedures!).

The simplest way of ensuring that induction training is completed comprehensively is to prepare a checklist. This might be divided into:

- introduction to the company, and
- introduction to the job.

A sample induction training checklist for sales staff is shown at the back of this chapter, and could be adapted for use in most businesses.

There is no reason why some of the induction task should not be delegated around the existing sales team – providing the manager is convinced that all team members are:

- confident that they are using the correct systems/policies
- capable of giving clear instruction to others.

In reality, most of this task is likely to be given to the senior team members to do – and it is essential that the manager takes overall control of the process (with mini-reviews with the 'learner' from time-to-time).

It is impossible to define here the duration of an induction programme. In some more simple sales roles it might be completed in a day or two. In other firms, a Sales Consultant may not have completed a fully structured programme inside six weeks. This process forms an essential part of the staff development of the newcomer.

Research shows that a major cause of labour turnover is failure to provide adequate induction training!

Case History

W L Gore & Associates, manufacturers of specialist fabric Goretex, uses a Sponsor system for the coaching of new employees. Their role goes much further than narrow induction issues and includes accomplishments, progress, well-being, problems and ambitions of the people being "sponsored". They also take an interest in the ways in which their charges are paid, through a committee structure in which they act as advocates for the people they sponsor. Sponsoring is not a new idea – but it requires training for the sponsors if top results are to be achieved.

Department store group, Bentalls Ltd., operate a sponsor system and thus ensure that structured training continues long after formal, off-the-job training is completed.

3. Reviewing performance

A driver setting off on a journey towards a rendezvous where a family party has been planned needs to know the route plan and how long it should take to get there. Along the way, time-checks will be made to see whether progress is sufficient to enable the deadline to be met. A recent advertisement comparing the kind of distractions which can occur in car travel (by comparison with travelling by rail) well illustrates the potential frustrations which can be experienced in traffic hold-ups, coffee breaks and through misreading the map! So it can be in business life and a regular review of progress towards those business goals is essential if all the players keep their 'eyes on the ball' all the time.

Reviewing performance should be the most natural activity for any manager to carry out!

On a day-by-day basis, mini-reviews are discussed:

'How has the day gone?' we may ask (or be asked).

'What kind of a week have we had?'

'How close are we to the target?'

Well-motivated team members will be very interested in the answers to these questions but they hardly constitute a full performance review. The difference lies in the time invested and focus of the discussion. 'What have we achieved?' is replaced by 'How well have you contributed to the team's performance and how can we help to improve that in the future?' In other words, the manager is reviewing the performance of each team member in the context of their own strengths and weaknesses, hopes and fears, likes and dislikes and trying to re-focus their efforts on how to achieve even better results.

Why does there seem to be a resistance to carrying out appraisals? There are many answers to this question. Mostly it is because of a fundamental misunderstanding about the nature and purpose of the task in hand. The process of reviewing performance is not a parallel with the visit to the Head Teacher – and, for maximum effectiveness, the conversation should not be a 'Telling' process. Much more effectively, the counselling style concentrates on asking the staff member what they think about their performance – and how it might be helped.

To be successful, performance reviews must be linked to standards or targets – or there will be no central focus for the discussion!

In the absence of a system which allows the individual's sales performance to be recorded and measured (e.g. through dissection on the till) a review can still be carried out – but performance can only be counselled as the strict measures will be missing (many managers make use of average sales results in such a case).

A frequently quoted complaint is that performance reviews are difficult to do because they take up so much time. This is a poor excuse. We have already seen that the selection interview is going to take a minimum of 30 minutes (at screening level) and possibly a further hour at shortlist level; is it too much to ask for the manager to devote a further hour of his undivided attention to his individual team members every six months or so? Failure to do this could be read as disinterest by team members ('The manager is only interested in us as a means of making money!' it might be said).

Finally, it is sometimes claimed by managers that, as the firm does not have a policy or procedure for performance reviews, they are not expected to be done. This argument is like saying that because the hosts at that family party did not send a map, we should not use one in helping us to arrive on time. Whole books have been written on this subject – especially on the design of a system and the supporting paperwork – but the most important aspects are that:

- a discussion takes place involving a review of the individual's performance
- adequate attention is given to individual strengths and weaknesses (with the aim of exploiting the strengths and overcoming any weak areas)
- the resulting record of the meeting should focus on a personal action plan in which the manager/organisation will support the individual's personal development (see next chapter on what this might include).

Sales staff do get stale from time-to-time and this important system provides one opportunity to help 're-texture' their sales approaches and energies; over a period of time, it will also help to document the track record of success for each team member.

Here is a checklist of points which need considering in preparing for a performance review:

Checklist: Preparing for a performance review

Prepare:

1. Give adequate notice of the meeting to your team members.
2. Consider their performance - last period's objectives and supporting facts.
3. Plan for privacy and adequate time.

Discuss:

4. Review what happened.
5. Explore why it happened.
6. Agree what should happen in the future (next objectives).

Follow-up:

7. Provide the necessary support to help the team member perform.
8. Review progress being made between appraisals.

4. Coaching

Coaching is the systematic development of an individual on a day-by-day basis – often benefiting from actual incidents at work which provide the opportunity for discussion and learning. The term 'coaching' is often confused with 'correction' and, whilst the two things aim to achieve the same result, coaching seeks to involve the team member in understanding why things are best done in a particular way – and helping them to make the change (correction may involve a lot of shouting and stamping!).

Successful coaches build up a close relationship with their 'learners' – compare this with the swimming coach (who will provide lots of encouragement to the learner – but usually from outside the swimming pool!), or the music teacher (who does a lot of listening and commenting, and may even demonstrate how the music should be performed). Direct results from coaching sessions can usually be directly identified – but only if the manager has correctly assessed the improvement target in the first instance.

There are a number of potential pitfalls in making the coaching of sales staff work successfully:

- **Observation is vital.** The manager needs to 'listen-in' on sales interviews to assess where the individual's strengths and weaknesses might lie. This needs to be done with great subtlety – avoiding any embarrassment with customers and the impression with staff that they are being 'checked-up' on.
- **Training requires follow-up.** It is pointless investing time with a team member trying to improve their selling skills if the manager fails to check on their subsequent progress. The approach should be: 'I was pleased to see that you closed that sale without any trouble – those techniques we discussed really do work, don't they?' or, 'You still seemed to have some difficulty with those features and benefits we talked about at the last training session, why not try the bridging statement: 'and that means...' next time? I think you'll find it flows better'.
- **Separating training from performance.** When you follow up previous training and coaching sessions, you sometimes find that people have a very odd idea of what training is supposed to be achieving. For example when suggesting a team member tries out that 'new idea' you discussed at last week's team meeting you may get the following response 'Oh, I didn't realise you actually wanted us to **do** it!'
- **Set a good example.** The credibility of the coach will always be tested when he or she fails to practise what he preaches. None of us has a monopoly of the 'best methods' and some sales people will always be successful although they seem to break some of the 'golden rules' and get away with it. However, your coaching influence will wane if:
  - you cannot practise what you are teaching, or
  - you demonstrate short patience,
  - there is a shortfall in your own product knowledge, or
  - your social skills are worn out!
- **'Them' and 'Us'.** When 'difficult' customers leave the shop, do you find yourself leading an inquisition on what went wrong – mainly attacking the customer. This can lead to a dangerous: 'We are the only ones in the right, here – it's the customers who are wrong' attitude. This can be detected in a variety of businesses which the reader might have visited as a customer.

- **Respect.** Coaches need to have the respect of their charges – and this is earned, not bought. It is an essential ingredient for coaching to work really well and depends upon the manager adopting correct behaviour in the business at all times.

Coaching provides a powerful force for improving individual performance and the principal investment from the manager is time!

5. Counselling

It is very unlikely that employees will be able to concentrate at work if they are currently going through some major trauma in their lives – or they feel that security in their jobs is being threatened. It may seem strange but worries and difficulties are not always fed back to the manager who has probably noticed that something is wrong – but cannot quite pinpoint the nature of the problem. It is easy to ignore such a situation – but this is generally not the best policy.

A close relationship between the manager and the team should ensure that, when it comes to problems, the manager is always willing to offer a listening ear and some support – if only to help the person remove some of the worst aspects of the 'hurt' so that they can concentrate on the job in hand.

Counselling has taken on quite a large role in society and the reader may be forgiven for feeling that it has become the province of the experts. Nothing could be further from the truth.

Managers are quite able to learn counselling skills and apply these in a variety of settings; this is particularly relevant when the purpose of the meeting is simply to discover what is wrong and how the owner of the problem can begin to come to terms with the problem.

For counselling to work successfully, the following 'techniques' should be practised:

Counselling checklist

Prepare for these stages:

1. Prepare the environment (confidential, discreet).
2. Clarify the objective of the meeting.
3. Decide specific investigation points.
4. Help with a constructive approach to solving the problem.
5. Plan a course of action.
6. Summarise your team member's decisions.

Develop your counselling skills:

Attention

1. Establish rapport - eye contact etc.
2. Use 'open behaviour' - nods, smiles etc.
3. recognise emotional behaviour.

Active listening

1. Use silence.
2. Observe body language/ behaviour.
3. Use general/open questions.
4. Take notes (if your team member approves).

Specific counselling skills

Try to use:

1. paraphrasing
2. open questions/probing technique
3. reflecting feelings
4. focusing on specific topics
5. summarising.

Counselling helps managers create a closer working relationship with individual team members especially if this support is forthcoming when team members most need it!

6. Grievances

Another cause of poor or erratic performance is through grievances – and the unfortunate fact is that most grievances are caused by the boss! Readers may not be able to imagine a situation where they have gone out of their way to upset a team member – and that is exactly what grievance procedures are for. They provide a guaranteed opportunity for the individual to complain about some aspect of the way they are being managed without fear of being singled out for further trouble.

The kinds of difficulties which can lead to grievances being aired are:

- rotas, lunch-breaks or holiday arrangements being changed without consultation
- development training or promotion being offered 'over the head' of the individual who thought they ought to have been given the chance to apply.

A standard procedure involves taking the problem which has caused the difficulty direct to your manager, who has the task of hearing it through and trying to resolve it. Generally, the employee is allowed to have a colleague (or staff representative) witness the meeting and its outcome. Managers are best advised to apologise if they feel that they might have contributed to any misunderstanding or difficulty. Failure to resolve the problem usually means that the 'plaintiff' may take the problem to the next level of management for a hearing – and so on up to the very top. This means that the first line manager will have to report on the first grievance meeting to prepare more senior managers for their meetings.

This might sound as though grievance procedures can just consume large amounts of time and emotional effort for little return.

Organisations that have introduced grievance procedures usually find that, unless there has been a matter of principle involved (e.g. an Equal Opportunities policy has not been seen to work), most difficulties leading to a grievance are quickly resolved at a local level and do not go any further 'up the ladder'!

Those matters of principle which do go the distance, often contribute to a review and change of an organisation's policies or practices.

Assignment

If your organisation has a published Grievance Procedure, take this opportunity of re-reading it and discuss its implications with your manager (who may also be able to brief you on past cases which have been resolved).

7. Discipline

Unfortunately, once-reliable staff sometimes go off the rails and the organisation has to have a system for dealing with such situations. Mostly, when trouble comes, it is in small doses and an informal warning is sufficient to stop it repeating. There is no hint here that a sledgehammer should be taken to a nut but even relatively small issues such as persistent lateness or taking a Saturday off as sick-leave (when the person is known to be well), can become a serious problem if it is not dealt with early on.

Most businesses have adopted a disciplinary procedure and have very tight control on who is allowed to issue warnings or take more serious disciplinary action. A typical system will define:

- situations in which a warning by the local manager may be required (e.g. the time keeping example above) – this would be an informal warning (but would need to be diarised or there would be no record of it taking place). The outcome of a meeting should be a clear statement of the behaviour gap which needs to be filled for the 'offence' to be deleted.
- persistent and continuing repetition would bring the threat of a written warning (the second stage); once again the clear statement of the performance gap needs to be agreed and the action needed to put the situation right. The offer of help from the manager should also be recorded.
- the final written warning – in some systems – may coincide with a notice of dismissal and, provided the employer has behaved reasonably throughout the sequence of events, the case is unlikely to 'blow-up'.

There is a great deal of misunderstanding about the law on unfair dismissal and the individual's recourse to an Industrial Tribunal. However, provided a disciplinary procedure exists and it has been properly followed, then a court case should not ensue.

At the most serious end of discipline lies the offence of gross misconduct and this also has to be defined in the organisation's policy. Gross misconduct could be theft, being drunk/drugged on duty, or fighting, and such 'offences' are usually met with instant dismissal. (In reality, there may be a need to build up a portfolio of evidence. The best 'intermediate' step would be to suspend the employee on full pay pending a full enquiry. This approach helps to ensure that irrevocable steps are not taken in the heat of the moment.).

It should be remembered throughout the consideration of disciplinary issues that there may be some external reason for uncharacteristic behaviour of the employee – and that, once this is uncovered, the meeting may turn into something quite different (probably a counselling meeting)!

Assignment

It is essential that all Sales Managers understand how their organisation's Disciplinary procedure works and, most importantly, their limits of authority (and how the firm expects records to be made). This assignment involves checking out the firm's Policy and Procedures and gaining a briefing on past cases involved in the firm.

Finally, it should be kept in mind that the first thought of the manager in a disciplinary case is not usually how to end the employment of a team member; rather it is to provide the means by which he or she might be encouraged to change their behaviour and return to the 'fold'!

8. Individual sales development

The reader will have noticed that most of the sections in this chapter have application in motivating team members to improve their performance. Mostly, we are able to improve our abilities once we have a determination to do so. However, there are many different approaches to helping people develop in their jobs, and here we have an opportunity to review the more practical of them:

Workplace experience and practice

Workplace experience provides a rich source of learning and behaviour modelling yet we probably underrate its importance. Sales people, particularly, learn a great deal from the sales conversations of colleagues around them and, if they are especially good, the behaviour modelling approach can be very effective. Unfortunately, the reverse can also be true, which is why 'on-the-job' training should be carefully controlled. Well established sales people will already have adopted their own styles of selling and should also have a command of the essential skills. However, less experienced sales people really need guidance and coaching from a trusted staff member – and the manager should have planned who should fill this role and ensured that the coach is properly briefed for it.

Distance learning

Following the advent of the Open University, there has been an enormous expansion of courses and learning materials – all designed to help busy people improve their capabilities and understanding of the business world (or parts of it). Today, learning aids are widely available on CD ROM – enabling those with access to a computer to be able to learn all manner of subjects and skills – and never leave their homes. Effective managers take a considerable interest in these applications as they offer an insight into the interests and aspirations of their staff.

The principal advantage of open or distance learning courses is that most of the work is carried out by learners under their own steam. However, there are usually progress tests and assignments for the learner to complete and, although distance learning is often thought of as a private matter, the manager can be very encouraging and supportive – or the very reverse. Any individual development should help a staff member contribute more at work and the good leader will look for ways in which this can be achieved. This does not necessarily mean helping staff gain promotion – the triangle gets narrower as you climb up the hierarchy. However, there are ways of contributing to the sales efforts of the team without moving out of selling (see above section). So, if you have a team member undertaking a distance learning course, you should ensure that you provide as much support as possible. Failure to take any interest at all may lead to the 'learner' seeing their own private study as a valuable route out of your organisation – and you may only find out about it second-hand or too late to influence the individual's decision.

(The bssa provides a wide range of open and distance learning programmes for busy retailers).

Private reading

There has been an enormous explosion of business books in the last ten years – and many of them have direct relevance to selling, influencing and interpersonal skills. As well as distance learning, team members can be encouraged to develop themselves through guided reading – again with the added support of the manager in discussing what has been learned from the text. (The Appendix includes a number of publications which could be used by coaches in helping team members with their individual development).

Job rotation

Rotating responsibilities in a business often sounds quite impossible but when the reader stops to think about this a little more deeply, the method is probably already used. Many retail businesses divide up responsibility for 'supervising' different stocks – or main classifications – in the business (i.e. price-marking, stock care, rotation, re-ordering, and merchandising) and this can help each person learn a great deal about the merchandise in 'their' section. The possible risks of rigidity in the team – arising from specialisation – can best be avoided by rotating these responsibilities from time-to-time. The long term outcome of this approach is that all the team will have developed 'all round' skills and knowledge (and in some depth!).

Delegation

As has been stated above, the 'pyramid' nature of most organisation charts restricts promotion opportunities. In some retail organisations this difficulty has been amplified by 'flatter' structures and the increasing empowerment of front-line sales staff. However, greater job satisfaction can be gained through the delegation of specific tasks which may previously have been seen as the task of a Supervisor – or even the manager.

Delegation, provided it is preceded by some training or coaching in the task being delegated, can be an effective way of improving the productivity of the team (and enabling the manager to concentrate on what he or she should really be doing – i.e. leading the sales team and motivating them to achieve sales and profit targets).

Most of us will remember how it felt to be trusted with a delegated task for the first time and, contrary to supposition, most team members welcome the insights into broader issues and responsibilities provided through delegation.

Secondment or attachment

Most of us have, at some time or another, been attracted by the 'grass in another field' only to discover that, when we have crossed over to investigate it more closely, it wasn't nearly as attractive as we had supposed. Some organisations take the view that team players who have only the direct experience of the one organisation may have insufficient experience to qualify for promotion. This can lead to promising staff leaving for a 'wider world' – and, unfortunately, they may not always return.

A route around this problem is to offer team members the opportunity of a temporary transfer into another department, section, or branch; with careful supervision of this kind of experience, it is amazing how much may be learned – including the fact that your team is better run than any other around!

Authorship

Does your business have a staff newsletter or journal? Do you have a member of your team who could contribute a short article (or even a regular column) on customer care issues? Writing is not everybody's skill but, whilst writing, it is amazing how much you remember about the subject – how you coped with specific customers, the surprises you had when they spent more than you expected – and the disappointments as well.

The fact that the article is written by a salesperson, more credibility should be attracted to the content, and your team will benefit from the enhanced reputation of having the author in your group.

9. Summary

Successful managers rarely need to rely upon the 'heavier' techniques listed in this chapter - in fact they would feel that they have failed if they have to invoke the disciplinary procedure. However, mistakes are made in life, unfortunately, and the firm must have a way of handling these difficulties.

Just now and again, we all stray from the narrow path and need a helping hand back onto it again. Perhaps this is another way of looking at the role of the manager - the person who tries to lead the team towards the firm's objectives, trying to help them stay on the correct path when there may be so many temptations on all sides!

In our next chapter we will look at one of the main causes for misunderstandings in business - Group Communications.

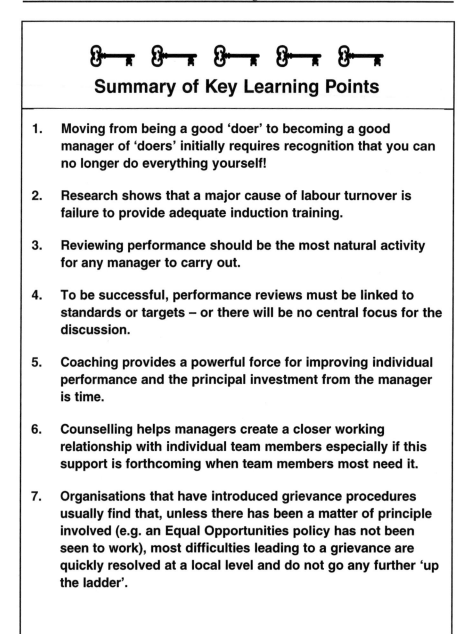

Summary of Key Learning Points

1. Moving from being a good 'doer' to becoming a good manager of 'doers' initially requires recognition that you can no longer do everything yourself!

2. Research shows that a major cause of labour turnover is failure to provide adequate induction training.

3. Reviewing performance should be the most natural activity for any manager to carry out.

4. To be successful, performance reviews must be linked to standards or targets – or there will be no central focus for the discussion.

5. Coaching provides a powerful force for improving individual performance and the principal investment from the manager is time.

6. Counselling helps managers create a closer working relationship with individual team members especially if this support is forthcoming when team members most need it.

7. Organisations that have introduced grievance procedures usually find that, unless there has been a matter of principle involved (e.g. an Equal Opportunities policy has not been seen to work), most difficulties leading to a grievance are quickly resolved at a local level and do not go any further 'up the ladder'.

Summary of Key Learning Points

8. It should be remembered throughout the consideration of disciplinary issues that there may be some external reason for uncharacteristic behaviour of the employee – and that, once this is uncovered, the meeting may turn into something quite different (probably a counselling meeting).

9. The first thought of the manager in a disciplinary case is not usually how to end the employment of a team member; rather it is to provide the means by which he or she might be encouraged to change behaviour and return to the 'fold'.

10. Managers can play a big part in encouraging individuals to develop their own skills and performance within the team using self-development methods; the investment will be minimal – but the pay-off considerable.

Sample induction checklist

The following checklist could be issued to the new joiner and signed off by each instructor as each unit is completed. This makes monitoring the programme much easier - it is then possible to review the success of the programme when it is complete.

		Instructors Initials
1	**Introduction to the Organization**	
1.1	Brief history of the company	
1.2	Trading policies	
1.3	Confirmation of employment contract (details)	
1.4	Hours and rotas/ what to do if absent from work	
1.5	Staff purchase scheme	
1.6	Arrangements for attendance/ absence	
1.7	Company rules - training, Health & Safety, discipline and grievance policies	
1.8	Security of personal possessions (handbags, etc.)	
1.9	Breaks	
2	**Introduction to the job**	
2.1	Department/ Branch layout (stock layouts)	
2.2	Dress code	
2.3	Names of Managers & colleagues	
2.4	Customer Care policy	
2.5	Terminal/ service desk/ till operation	
2.6	Product knowledge	
2.7	'Signature' system (for authorisations)	
2.8	Goods Received system - safety & security	
2.9	Accident & fire evacuation procedures	
2.10	End of trading-day procedures	
3	**Basic job training**	
3.1	Visual merchandising	
3.2	Re-cap: acceptance of payments - credit cards, cheque validation, etc. (Systems)	
3.3	Selling Skills - 9 steps to a sale	
3.4	Basic stock ordering systems (basics & special orders)	
3.5	Special services - measuring/estimation, alterations, deliveries, etc.	
3.6	Stock rotation and stockroom control	
3.7	Security procedures - cash, stock etc.	
3.8	Wastage control	
3.9	Complaints policy	
3.10	Customer database system	
4	**Development**	
4.1	Advanced selling skills	
4.2	In-depth product knowledge	
4.3	Fire warden training	
4.4	First-aider training	

5

Group Communication and Training

How to steer the team towards your goals and targets

1. Introduction

We have already seen that good Sales Managers cannot spend all their time on the shop floor, leading the sales effort. Quite apart from anything else, the selection process will take up quite some time, even if the business has specialist personnel and training staff to help.

As we progress through this book, it will become increasingly obvious that managers need to manage by doing manager's work. This means that they need to trust their teams to get on with their jobs whilst the manager...

- plans
- organises, and
- forecasts

... the next round of business activities. Failure to do this will jeopardise the continuing growth and development of the team – and may ultimately lead to a whirlpool of crisis management!

This chapter will consider how to use the following:

- briefing groups
- in-store training sessions
- training methods
- brainstorming.

2. Group communications

Despite the most modern methods available to us, it seems that the most difficult thing to achieve inside a firm is good communications. Come to think of it, communications are difficult to maintain in families and in social clubs ... perhaps this has something to do with the one common factor – *human beings*?

It is possible to make progress and improve this most vital factor in business but only by making an extra special effort at getting it right! The thing is, people love to have a good gossip. Most large organisations (and some small ones?) have a very healthy grapevine in which speculation is rife and 'fishy tales' grow in direct relationship to the lack of official statements.

Even when good systems for communications exist in the organisation, people still find ways of getting round them and line managers, especially, have an important role in ensuring that downward messages are accurately conveyed and upward feedback is also communicated. The test of an efficient communications system lies in the speed and uniformity of a decision taken at Board level and the subsequent implementation of that decision in the firm's local unit. Yet there is plenty of documentary evidence of communications going wrong – the commonest alibi is *'But I thought that I told you!'* – and, even if the telling process was done, was there any guarantee that the 'audience' was listening?

A first priority for managers is to ensure that all members of their team are kept up to date with the 'big picture' of their organisations. They can only do this if they, too, make a point of keeping up-to-date!

3. Briefing groups

Policy decisions are taken in all businesses from time to time and it is important that these are communicated down the line in such a way that everyone receives the same message at more or less the same time. Some organisations issue a formal, written brief and cascade the information down the line with managers trained to present the information in such a way that the policy information is clearly understood by all. (Middle managers have a particular responsibility to get this right as they have to take the data on to their own meetings where they may receive queries from their own local managers – and they need to be able to handle these professionally or the system may lose some credibility).

Some information which is disseminated in this way will be 'Company Confidential' and it is important that this is observed (generally speaking, staff will be trustworthy if they are trusted!).

Case History – 'Lifts have ears!'

A major London department store enjoyed a very virile grapevine which was fuelled by the lift attendants. One of their 'stations' was close to the Boardroom and, unfortunately some Board meetings had a tendency to continue into the lift. This encouraged the Drivers to 'add two and two together' and a speculative version of the discussion was quickly dispatched around the store. Such methods can be very damaging and it took quite a long time before the 'leak' was discovered!

A version of the briefing game is adopted in many independent, as well as national businesses – and the practice of starting the day with 'company prayers' has been adopted by many department managers. The aim here is for managers to concentrate the team's thoughts or expectations for the day (and possibly the day's targets), tasks which will be needed to be undertaken, visitors expected during the day and possibly new deliveries arriving (where these are known). A short 10-15 minute briefing every morning can be exceptionally valuable and welcomed by team members. It is sometimes felt that this method has limited value when so many sales staff are part-timers and may not be present for the brief. The simplest way of overcoming this is to delegate the task to brief them to one or two full-time team members (e.g. Assistant Manager and/or Sales Team Leader).

Case History

Independent department store, Williams and Griffin of Colchester, adopted Briefing Groups in 1990 and the method has been operating virtually ever since. What is noticeable from a tour of the store at around opening time is that the staff are deep in concentration as they are briefed on the plans for the week. Confidential attitude surveys of the store's staff reveal that they highly value this well established method of keeping them in the picture; the time is obviously so well invested that some department managers have extended the method so that briefing groups are run every morning.

It is important that the Briefing Group method is not seen simply as one-way communication and that an appropriate mechanism is used for upward feedback, too!

4. In-store training

Training may not always be considered to be part of the communications system – but it doubtless provides opportunities to open up discussion – and anything that does that, helps towards improving communication in the organisation.

However, training sessions should aim to achieve more than communicating one person's or department's view of what needs to be done. To be effective, a training session should aim to improve the knowledge, skills or attitudes of the team and this will be achieved if the session leader has planned the session correctly. This will be easier when the manager has been trained in Instructional Techniques and has the skill of planning and delivering a group training session.

The main variation between a truly effective and an indifferent training session lies in the quality of preparation which has preceded it. 7/8ths of the training time should be invested in preparation!

5. The lesson plan

At first sight, running a training session for half an hour may look a daunting prospect to the new manager but, if the plans are made well and the team responds well to the topic, the time may actually prove to be very tight.

How can 30 minutes be found for such a session anyway? Since 1970, many firms have operated a Training Half-Hour policy every week – starting at 8.45a.m., with the shop opening late at 9.15 or even 9.30 (on the quietest day of the week).

A 'Lesson Plan' for each training session (as taught on the training course mentioned above) is a helpful way of ensuring that the time is profitably used and the session truly memorable!

The first step is to set some training objectives and then to plan out the detailed shape for the session. This should include:

- **Introduction** (2-3 minutes setting out the need for the topic)
- **Instruction** (4-5 minutes setting out the 'golden rules')
- **Demonstration/Illustration** (7-8 minutes showing how it should be done.)
- **Practicals** (7-8 minutes of practical work by the group)
- **Discussion** (2-3 minutes discussing any difficulties/revelations etc)
- **Summary** (2-3 minutes re-cap of the 'Golden Rules')

The art of making such a session truly effective is to ensure that it has some vivid effect – particularly through the use of visual aids. These do not need to be sophisticated. Photographs cut out from trade magazines or the newspaper can provide illustrations of happy and miserable faces (useful for a session on Customer Approach) and, if you have a video player available, a selected extract from your favourite TV soap may illustrate a typical misunderstanding between people (useful as a demonstration of the importance of clear communication between customers and salespeople.).

Participants also like to be able to participate – their natural reserve will quickly disappear when it is apparent that training sessions can be fun, so it is important to build in some practical exercises (for example, role playing on how to close the sale). Finally, some simple flip-chart sheets (e.g. mounted on a large cardboard box) will provide a simple visual aid and a central focus for the key points from the Session.

So, let us re-cap on that Lesson Plan format listed above and turn it into a real session on Approaching Customers – starting with the objectives.

Training objective

By the end of the training session, participants will:

- know the company's policy on customer approach and
- be able to put it into practice with all visitors to the business.

It may also be helpful to write down the main purpose of the session – bearing in mind the mixed experience of the group. For example, the session will be a re-cap for some members, and a new topic for the recent joiners – both groups need to be involved.

Sales Training

TITLE: 'CUSTOMER APPROACH'

STAGE	NOTES	AIDS
INTRODUCTION (2/3 minutes)	A recent personal experience on a shopping trip: questions on what the group thought of the experience.	Title Page Training Objectives Questions on Chart
INSTRUCTION (4/5 minutes)	'Golden Rules' the company wants staff to follow: 1 Be 'customer aware' 2 Smile/ greet within 1 minute of entry 3 Use open questions 4 Observe body language 5 Look for opportunities for intervention.	Illustration of Rules Captions & Graphics
DEMONSTRATION (7/8 Minutes)	Role-play showing both the 'wrong' way - then the 'right' way.	Group member prepared for the role-play - as a typical custome trainer provides staff roles; or two pieces of contrasting video used - Group encouraged to provide criticism.

PRACTICE (7/8 minutes)	Group divided in 'threes', 1 customer 1 sales person, 1 observer. Given three exercises to carry out. Rotate the roles.	Three role--play briefs: 1 'just-looking' customer 2 abrupt customer in hurry 3 really choosy customer needing advice
DISCUSSION (3/4 minutes)	Open up discussion of the exercises: - 'How did they work'? Ask development questions, e.g.: - 'Would this work on the first day of the Sales? - 'What would you do if you were already serving a customer?	Prepared questions and model answers on flip-chart.
SUMMARY (2/3 minutes)	Re-cap 'Golden Rules', adding any development points arising out of the exercises or discussion. e.g.: 'As we saw...' End with snappy punchline, e.g.: 'Remember, Customer Approach either counts you IN - or counts you OUT!'	Caption of 'Rules' on chart. Punchline on chart.

Assignment

Now that you have seen how the Lesson Plan can be used, prepare your own version for another Selling Skills or Customer Care subject which you could then use with your team in the near future.

5. Evaluation of training

Evaluating training is a notoriously difficult task – training is probably better viewed as an 'Act of Faith' rather than an item which can be tested like an element of financial appraisal. The manager should be able to judge whether the training sessions have proved worthwhile simply by observing how team members have been applying the contents of the training sessions in their daily lives. Failure to witness any change will bring the reaction that perhaps the group was 'deaf'! Certainly, it will be valuable to follow up the sessions and find out why the results were disappointing (remember the Coaching parable in Chapter 4 – 'Oh, I didn't realise you wanted us to *do* it!').

Reaction to training is something which is easier to measure and the following feedback form could provide some useful feedback for the manager running in-house training sessions. Good times to use this device would be after, say, the first session of a series (when there is still time to change things) and again towards the end of a series (when the participants will be better able to review the effects in the longer term.

Although 'happiness forms' such as this are often ridiculed, they do provide valuable feedback and in a form which makes the participants think about the training they have received.

Another aspect of continuing improvement is obtaining feedback on the session leader's own skills (which is also another reason for undertaking a Train the Trainer course). It would be useful to invite a more senior colleague or manager to 'sit-in' on a training session and ask them to provide feedback using the following critique.

Sales training review form

1. How relevant was the training to:

	your job	you personally
Fully relevant	❑	❑
Mostly relevant	❑	❑
Not very relevant	❑	❑

2. The pace of the training was:
   - ❑ rather fast
   - ❑ about right
   - ❑ rather slow

3. Three things I learned from the training were:
   a) ______________________________
   b) ______________________________
   c) ______________________________

3. Three things I plan to put into practice are:
   a) ______________________________
   b) ______________________________
   c) ______________________________

3. How could the trainer improve the training?
   a) ______________________________
   b) ______________________________
   c) ______________________________

Instructor critique sheet

for sales trainers

1. Was the trainer: ❑ approachable and easy to follow?
 ❑ mostly clear?
 ❑ confusing?

2. Did the trainer:

gain interest/attention at the start	Yes/No
... was it maintained throughout?	Yes/No
give the group a reason for the session?	Yes/No
present ideas logically?	Yes/No
provide illustrations/demonstrations?	Yes/No
involve the audience?	Yes/No
use open questions to test and involve?	Yes/No
emphasise key points in the session?	Yes/No
use the time well?	Yes/No
maintain fluency throughout?	Yes/No
project well to all the group and maintain audience contact?	Yes/No
use a friendly style?	Yes/No

Vivid training is an aim which every In-Store Trainer should aim for, and this is especially important for sales training sessions!

6. Training methods

Methods which could be used to achieve the 'vivid training' effect include:

- Role play exercises
- Case studies
- Video and audio materials
- Quizzes

- Competitions
- Comparison shopping exercises

Role play exercises

With typical British reserve, many people find the prospect of role playing intimidating – to have to 'act' in front of others somehow seems 'unreal', 'false', 'embarrassing'. The fact is that most sales people have to be able to use their personality and attributes in influencing customers – which sometimes means behaving in a less-than-usual way.

Role playing is a useful method for practising selling skills in a 'no risk' situation (that is, any mistakes will not lose any business, upset any customers or cause any lawsuits!)!

With the support of a colleague as an observer, an objective critique is also possible – especially if some kind of observation form is used to help facilitate some feedback. Role-play will work well when brief written notes are prepared for the 'customer' to follow – but this should stop short of a full script (after all, in everyday life, we are all customers as well!).

Case studies

It is amazing just how much effort learners are prepared to invest in discussing and agreeing possible courses of action arising from a well written, true-to-life case study. This method is less useful with team members who have only limited experience of the topic but, as a review method at the end of a piece, or series of training sessions, the method has much to commend it.

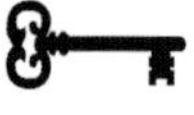

It should be remembered that Case Studies rarely have one single 'right' answer – and provide more of a test of the participants' ability to think through the possible routes to a solution!

A typical Case Study follows which could be re-written into the 'language' of most retail businesses.

Case Study

Mrs Longworth visited our shop three months ago on the first day of the Sale and, while hesitating over the choice of a very unusual three-piece suite (in mauve moquette!), was angered to discover that another salesman had sold the suite 'from under her nose'. Her demands to see the manager were lost in the general confusion and she eventually left muttering about writing a complaints letter to the MD. In fact, she returned on the following Monday and demanded an order to be placed for the same suite (which was still available – but on a rather unreliable delivery schedule).

The salesperson gained the manager's agreement that the order would be marked up at the Sale price and the order was placed with a request made for an 8-week delivery date. At precisely 8 weeks, the customer visited the shop again and demanded to know what had happened to her suite. The original salesperson (who had failed to track the order), had left the firm in the meantime and a colleague had the task of explaining that, while 8 weeks had been quoted, it was likely it would take a further 4 weeks to arrive. The customer became 'ballistic' and demanded a return of her 20% deposit and a full letter of apology from the firm. The sales person, in his embarrassment, issued an immediate refund of the £400 and tried his hardest to pacify the customer.

After the customer had gone and he had spent some hours of searching the order book and records, a scrappy note was discovered – pinned to the notice board in the manager's office – recording that the customer had demanded an order be placed. No record could be found of any deposit being paid, or an address ... two weeks after the last incident, the hideous suite arrived at the shop.

Assignment

- **Please discuss the service which this customer received from us and which procedures were ignored (if any).**
- **How should each of the 'players' have handled the customer and her order, to ensure that she was satisfied and the shop did not incur such a major loss?**
- **What action would you advise to be taken now?**

Video and audio materials

We are exceptionally fortunate in this decade to have access to such an amazing variety of visual and audio materials and, whilst amateur film-making is not recommended (from the sheer time investment viewpoint) there are many programmes shown on scheduled television (or on radio) which show scenes set in retail or service-centred organisations. With a little patience, it should be possible to illustrate all kinds of interpersonal skills (or lack of them!) from such small extracts. Just one word of warning – please do not be tempted to copy professional video tapes – or show your 'extracts' to large of groups of people – you may be infringing the copyright laws.

Audio tapes can bring the same effects – and, once again, it is surprising just how much effort groups will put into discussing scenarios which were quite obviously 'set up' as training scenes.

Audio and video illustrations provide vivid learning opportunities for your team and it is important that such aids correctly emphasise the desired knowledge and skills planned in the training session!

Quizzes

With so many quiz nights run these days in pubs and clubs, people have become more used to taking part in competitive quizzes. The process of compiling a battery of specific/factual questions may be very time-consuming, but the learning which can take place – simply by taking part in the activity, can be exceptionally rewarding. To make the session go really well, an attractive prize is recommended (perhaps a supplier may be prepared to sponsor this?). For guidance, see opposite.

Competitions

Training competitions can provide wider impact for the company's sales team and, for bigger competitions, effectiveness will probably be greater if they are run on a company-wide basis. (Competition between branches may heighten the effort which branch staff might put into the exercise and the only divisive issue may be how to accommodate non-selling staff in the competition). Again, a quality prize needs to be sought in order to motivate participation.

Quizzes - You will need some very precise rules – here are some suggestions on how to make the quiz successful:

- One person acts as Quizmaster (whose judgement is final).
- Another judges which team is the first to alert the quizmaster, when they are able to answer a competitive question
- Teams could be 2 or 3 members strong
- If the competitive question is answered correctly, the team may have 4 more questions before the next competitive question.

Correct answers for competitive questions bring 3 points, subsequent questions score 2 points each. Incorrect answers may be offered to other team(s) to answer at the discretion of the Quizmaster. A further competitive question then follows.

Comparison shopping

Whilst the prime objective of comparison shopping is generally not to provide training for those carrying it out, a comparison mission can be a valuable learning experience for all concerned. Making comparisons about prices and related qualities of product offered by competitors is essential market intelligence for any business – but in retailing, the impact of presentation and quality of service can be almost as vital.

Case History

A famous restaurant owner in America provides his staff with a budget – once a month – to take a meal in a competitor's restaurant. The only condition is that they report to him afterwards with a full analysis of the quality (value for money) and the quality of the service experienced. He maintains that, apart from the obvious information he gains about his competitors, this investment also provides a valuable impetus for his team to provide constant improvements in their customer service. The investment costs less than £50 per month and provides a return many times that value.

From the retailing perspective, a comparison shopping survey should be preceded by some revision training for the team on the key standards which your company is seeking in its own operations. These standards could then form the basis of an 'Observers' Report' to be used as the foundation for a subsequent de-briefing session. An example of this approach follows:

Sample Observer's Report

1	How 'customer aware' were the staff?	Very/ not very/ completely unaware?
2	Were you acknowledged/ greeted:	Immediately/ Too slowly/ Not at all?
3	Was the greeting/ approach:	Friendly/ formal/ warm/ non-existent?
4	How busy was the shop/ store?	Quiet/ some browsers/ very busy?
5	As a browser, did you feel you would be able to obtain adequate advice and assistance?	Yes/No
6	In your enquiry to a staff member, was your approach handled:	Reluctantly/ unconvincingly/ efficiently?
7	If you made a purchase, were you offered:	Related merchandise/ after sales service/ nothing?
8	How impressed were you by your visit:	Would not return/ might return to browse/ would definitely return to buy

Most impressive product(s)/ service(s):

1 ______________________________ Price £ ____________
2 ______________________________ Price £ ____________

Service factors I have learned from this visit:

1 ____
2 ____

The process of comparison is a valuable tool for all managers to use in the constant drive to maintain and improve sales and service standards!

7. Brainstorming

Group training sessions will be much more exciting when the team is encouraged to participate – and even compete with each other. One way of doing this is through the use of brainstorming which is a competitive technique for generating positive ideas. The method is valuable for leaders in a wide variety of fields – business and social – and can be used to encourage positive thinking (reducing negative thinking in a team) and for problem-solving.

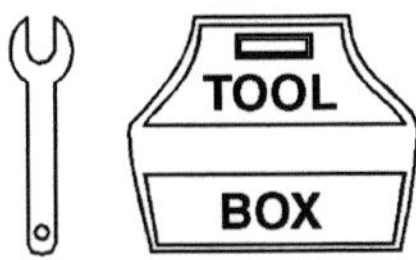

Successful brainstorming generally consists of two rounds – a dummy run preceding the main session and then the main session itself. The practice session is designed to form the right constructive mood for the meeting – and to set the rules. The main rule is that, while ideas are being generated, no one is allowed to promote negative ideas (or say things like "that's rubbish" or "that won't work"). Each session is followed by an evaluation of the ideas captured when some of the less worthwhile ideas may be excluded from the list (this needs great care as, sometimes, the craziest ideas turn out to be the most valuable.). All that is needed in the way of equipment is a flip-chart, a couple of felt-tip pens and a facilitator who has the ability to motivate the ideas from the Group.

The whole idea of brainstorming is that, when groups are motivated to be creative, there are few limits to the level and quality of ideas which are forthcoming!

(This is well illustrated in the film 'Apollo 13' when a technical support team was given a box of spare parts – available to the crew on the crippled ship – and told to brainstorm a way of re-generating oxygen for the crew. The outcome looked most unworkable as a structure – but it worked and contributed to the survival of the crew.)

Brainstorming as a technique has been credited with a number of profit generators, for instance:

- the invention of 'Post-it' pads arose from a meeting to discuss an adhesive which failed.
- Another famous meeting threw up an idea to increase the diameter of the nozzle in the toothpaste tube. Profits soared!

Assignment

A brainstorming session could work well as a means of generating ideas to promote an increase in sales. First of all, the group will need a "warm-up" session; this could encourage as many ideas for the use of a pencil as possible – listed on a flipchart – and then briefly reviewed. (You should aim for a total of, say, 30 ideas – before attempting to evaluate the suggestions.) The group should then be given a short relaxation before the title of the main session is given.

The main session then follows and, once again, all ideas (regardless of how sensible or not they seem to be) are recorded on the chart. Ideas generation should be encouraged to be "fast and furious" – the more competition between members of the group the better the results will be.

Once again, evaluation of the ideas normally takes place at the end of the session with a superimposed framework – e.g. categorising the "solutions" into:

- Short-term • Medium-term • Long-term...or
- Inexpensive • Mid-range • Costly

Care should be taken not to leave participants with the impression that no investment can be made at all – but obviously the real "pearls" will be those which come from maximum return for least investment.

8. Summary

This chapter has sought to remind the reader of the positive ways in which the team may be encouraged – through improved communication, motivation and the generation of positive ideas.

It is amazing what quite ordinary people can achieve in times of crisis – the distribution of creativity is wide in the community, it is just that this quality is often not encouraged or exploited in the workplace!

Time invested in these functions is rarely wasted, and will help to keep your team:

- well motivated
- enthusiastic
- creative, and
- productive!

Summary of Key Learning Points

1. **A first priority for all managers is to ensure that all members of their team are kept up-to-date with the 'big picture' of their organisations. They can only do this if they, too, make a point of keeping up-to-date.**

2. **It is important that the Briefing Group method is not seen simply as one-way communication and that an appropriate mechanism is used for upward feedback, too.**

3. **The main variation between a truly effective and an indifferent training session and lies in the quality of preparation which has preceded it. 7/8ths of the training time should be invested in preparation.**

4. **A 'Lesson Plan' for each training session is a helpful way of ensuring that the time is profitably used and the session truly memorable.**

5. **Vivid training – using all the senses of the participants – is an aim which every In-Store Trainer should aim for, and this is especially important for sales training sessions.**

6. **Role Playing is a useful method for practising selling skills in a 'no risk' situation (that is, any mistakes will not lose any business, upset any customers or cause any lawsuits!).**

7. **Case Studies rarely have one single 'right' answer – and provide more of a test of the participants' ability to think through the possible routes to a solution.**

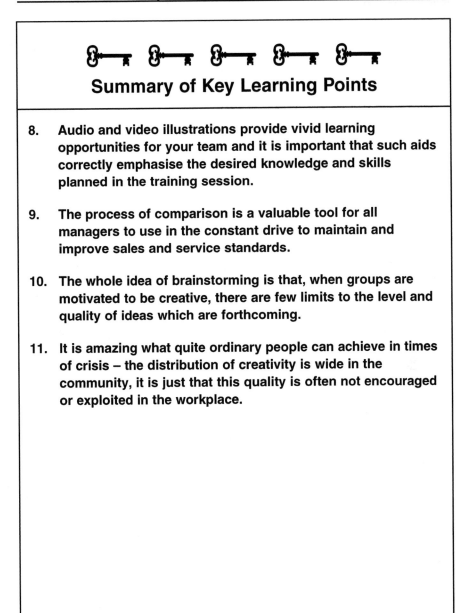

Summary of Key Learning Points

8. Audio and video illustrations provide vivid learning opportunities for your team and it is important that such aids correctly emphasise the desired knowledge and skills planned in the training session.

9. The process of comparison is a valuable tool for all managers to use in the constant drive to maintain and improve sales and service standards.

10. The whole idea of brainstorming is that, when groups are motivated to be creative, there are few limits to the level and quality of ideas which are forthcoming.

11. It is amazing what quite ordinary people can achieve in times of crisis – the distribution of creativity is wide in the community, it is just that this quality is often not encouraged or exploited in the workplace.

PART TWO

MANAGING CUSTOMER SERVICE

'Customers expect service. I will guarantee that any survey taken today of (rank and file) customers will tell you that the selling service in the stores in this country is poor. I shop all over the world, and this is not just an American problem. It's a problem in retail businesses everywhere.

'The store needs a floor manager with the time and responsibility to supervise sales ... not back in the corner working on time schedules or making out a report.'

Stanley Marcus
(Chairman Emeritus of Nieman-Marcus, Dallas, USA.)

6

Culture of the Business

From 'contempt' to highly motivated teams

1. Introduction

'The kind of 'riff-raff' we get in here...' as Basil Fawlty (in the award-winning 'Fawlty Towers') described his clientele to his wife and partner, told us more about his attitude towards business than about his actual customers. The success of the films may also reveal that many people have a sneaky regard for Maitre d'Hôtel, Fawlty, for being prepared to put into words things that we may have only had the temerity to think! However, his chaotic hotel – and its anti-customer antics – sadly reflect an attitude which is still to be found in some retail businesses.

Why should this be? Here are three possible reasons:

- **Rudeness**

  Much as service staff may claim to like working with people, members of the public can be exceptionally 'difficult' at times. In service roles, staff members can be on the receiving end of patronising, ill-mannered, aggressive and unspeakably rude behaviour. (This is not intended as a 'superior' statement – anyone with just 2-3 weeks' experience on the shop floor of a busy shop or store will appreciate what can be experienced.).

- **Boredom**

  Consistent service standards are difficult to achieve. Try as we might to maintain a fresh approach to every customer, it can be very difficult to make repeated phrases sound fresh – even more so when customers do not appear to value the effort taken.

Despite frequent denials and disbelief, most managers would agree that they have heard their front-line staff speak to customers in ways that caused their toes to 'curl up'!

- **Arrogance**

  The business culture may be 'anti-customer'. In other words, customers are seen (and may even be described behind the scenes) as 'punters', 'cannon-fodder' or even 'walking wallets' – and looked on as people who are 'fair game' to be 'ripped off', 'stitched-up' or otherwise 'taken advantage of'. It is very easy for this atmosphere to be projected right through the business – even if one wonders why customers fall into the traps!

This chapter explores reasons why such attitudes and cultures exist, and how they may be broken down.

2. 'Thinly disguised contempt'

When you think about it, this just about sums up some of the worst examples of appalling treatment which is meted out to customers by poorly run businesses and organisations. The expression – coined by guru Tom Peters – aptly describes that attitude which we can detect when the train announcement blames the delay on 'the wrong sort of snow' or even 'leaves on the line'. Does the apology sound credible to the passenger – or even to the speaker? Probably not, but this is the problem – the train inspector probably doesn't care. And whose fault is this?

Managers set the tone of the organisation when it comes to service standards – and they can become really good at that when they know that its results are measured and appreciated by their bosses!

So how is it that top management can take their eye off this particular ball?

At one level, the blame is laid at the feet of time – not enough of it; 'they' (the line managers) should know what they are doing, because they are paid by results – the focus of the business is to make a 'quick buck' – and everyone knows this; the business is 'peopled by experts' who have an ill concealed dislike of anyone who does not know what they know.

Is customer service a real priority in your business – so much so that everyone will put themselves out for a customer – even when they suspect there may not be a sale resulting from the contact? And are those priority standards shared across the organisation with a rigorous consistency? For example, have all customer contact staff received training in the standards which your organisation requires to be met at the customer interface? Or is this kind of training given an obvious 'back-seat' in favour of more exotic activities? Just how much sales and customer care training have you received? And your *team*?

A mini-survey of delegates on 1-day and 2-day selling and customer care training workshops has revealed just how little formal training many sales people have received on these subjects. So, is it any surprise that people 'make it up as they go along', learn on the job, and often get it wrong. But they may be led by managers who are no better trained or prepared!

In discussions at customer care workshops, participants tell us of occasions when service standards have slipped, through:

- breakdowns in systems – a special order system failed and the customer was not informed that the product requested is now obsolete or de-listed

- a customer is not informed early enough about a service failure – causing a delay and a wasted journey (a telephone call would have saved the customer's time)
- a staff member – obviously enjoying the company of a previous customer – turns off the charm for the next one
- a customer needing some information is told to 'wait his turn' when he seeks a small piece of advice
- the barman who can only seem to see the well dressed customers queuing at his bar – the others are 'invisible'
- the refusal to make a 'special case' for a customer who has genuinely missed a deadline for a very good reason.

Ultimately, consistent service standards is what separates the key players in a market from the rest – for example:

- the Price Promise offered by John Lewis on all non-food products throughout the network of stores
- the 'no fuss' return guarantee offered by Argos up to 16 days after purchase
- consistent 'value-for-money' merchandise quality standards achieved by Marks and Spencer throughout their ranges
- the British Gas commitment to a minimum call-out time in emergency cases
- McDonald's' rigorous policy on cleanliness and uniform service standards
- British Airways' determination to be punctual.

These are just a few examples of the good ones – the companies whose very names have become a by-word for the policies they provide. But in each case, the policy would not be effective without the professional handling of the customer, which should always accompany the experience.

There is no point in having a 'no fuss' refund policy if, when the customer takes up her right to it, she finds that the staff either resent/disbelieve her story or they are simply incompetent and cannot carry out the policy!

So, how should the messages be conveyed to customers?

- By using the right words. If you must ask 'How can I help?' – why not try – 'How ***may*** I help?' – it actually means something different.
- Using an appropriate tone of voice – soft? sweet? smiling? relaxed? All these tones will encourage the customer to want to work with you
- Using the right body language – not bored, aggressive or flirtatious, but positive, open, strong (eye contact), and keeping the negative body movements under control (e.g. shrugs, nodding head, etc.).

Here is the subject for another group training session (see chapter 6).

Thinly disguised contempt (TDC) should be replaced with explicitly proud delight (EPD) that customers should want to use our business!

3. Negative staff attitudes

From time to time, some of the following attitudes may be identifiable from individuals in your business, and the resulting challenge to your leadership should not pass without an appropriate comment. See how many of them you have heard or have been implied in the actions of your team:

'The customer should wait on us as they need our advice.'

'I must just finish checking this invoice before I offer that customer help.'

'I suppose I had better go and help out on the Service Desk – they are a bit busy – but I really hate it.'

'I love a good argument over a customer complaint – most customers haven't a clue about washing instructions, or anything else.'

'Those customers are only filling in time – you watch, they'll pick up a few things then wander off.'

'There are plenty more customers where they came from; who do these people think they are?'.

The fact that customers may not respond or reciprocate those extra vocal and non-verbal touches described above, does not entitle anyone to 'drop their guard' and allow their service standards to fall.

Managers play an important part in helping to keep customer service standards high!

4. Positive attitudes

Our attitudes are affected by our:

- mood
- how well we are treated
- things that happen before we get to work
- how we are treated by customers (and colleagues)
- our ability to resist negative thinking by being positive.

Positive attitudes are affected in staff by the level of motivation which has been encouraged by the organisation in general, and the manager in particular!

The use of the following checklist may help managers encourage team members to think about their behaviour and the impact they can have.

Checklist

Does my behaviour:

- give the customer a lasting and correct impression?
- give the customer confidence?
- reflect the company's policy and image?
- deal with the customer's queries and problems?
- build customer goodwill by encouraging customers to return?

Successful customer service staff quickly develop the skill of self-reflection – the ability to recognise their own strengths and weaknesses – and work on the improvement points themselves. Good managers encourage and assist with this process!

Case History

As part of a Training Half-Hour session, a manager asked the team to help produce a questionnaire which they could use (for themselves) to use as a self-checking device. The following items were selected and used as the basis for several training sessions which she went on to run for the team. At the end of this period, each sales person took a copy of the Checklist and used it on a regular basis to monitor their standards (some pairing was also used whereby one colleague checked another).

The above Case History illustrates the application of two principles:

- empowering the team to take ownership of the service criteria
- delegating the monitoring of the standards (with the manager acting as the 'long stop').

The agreed checklist covered:

- Did I obtain/use the customer's name? Yes/No
- What kind of business was the customer seeking? ____________
- What was the purpose of the purchase? ____________________
- Did I sell additional items? Yes/No
- Was I as helpful as I should have been? Yes/No
- Did I offer an Account? Yes/No
- Did I secure future business? Yes/No
- Have I passed on relevant information to my colleagues? Yes/No

The Case History cited satisfies one of the most basic rules of motivation:

If you want people to apply a new system or approach, first encourage them to help invent it; ownership comes from involvement!

There are other methods, as we shall see in the next Section.

5. Methods of motivation

It is sometimes argued that salespeople need to be 'hungry' for them to focus sufficiently on every customer to the point of concluding a sale. This theory would parallel a reward system whereby the employee is paid a very low basic wage (or perhaps none at all) but can then earn a substantial commission rate against achievement of sales targets.

It can also be argued that, in periods of 'plenty' such systems can over-reward when customers may not have required too much effort – but the worst effects would be noticed in recessionary periods when business might almost dry up (and the employee's income with it!).

Motivation, how to measure it and apply it, is worthy of a book on its own since many of the theories which have been applied to industry and employment can be argued in a variety of directions.

As we have seen above, in one 'corner' runs the argument that, if you want sales people to perform properly, they need to be given a share of the benefits which they are helping to achieve. In the other 'corner' is the argument that people perform better when their livelihood is not under constant threat or pressure and that they will achieve better results when they are able to use 'softer selling' methods. It is also argued that commission systems create a 'dog-eat-dog' atmosphere in the team where the better (or more aggressive) sales people don't mind what they do to grab customers from their more junior (or non-assertive) colleagues.

In reality, both arguments have their strengths and weaknesses but:

Whichever approach to motivation and reward is adopted, the atmosphere and culture of the business will have been affected in a major way!

For example, if the business operates in an aggressive marketing culture – with high commission payments – only sales staff who enjoy the 'thrill of the kill' will survive in it and it may be quite hard to find staff who are prepared to invest much time in the essential non-selling tasks in the business. Alternatively, the high basic salary business may attract staff who are rather 'laid-back' – happy in the knowledge that, if they are liked (or their product knowledge is valued) by the customer they will eventually make the sale.

Somewhere in the middle of the two arguments is the 'best of both worlds' whereby the team is motivated by the achievement of sales branch/department targets and rewarded with a percentage bonus on performance achieved above the target. (A variation of this approach has been promoted in recent years by HM Government through the Profit Related Pay method – enshrined in bonus payments based on the profit earned by the unit – or the Company as a whole).

The line manager is usually confronted with these systems as a 'fait accompli' – without the ability to affect the system of reward in the company. However:

It should always be remembered that, whilst money is a most important motivator, it is not the only one!

Maslow's 'Hierarchy of Needs' theory of motivation has long been applied in this area. It identifies progressive levels of motivation:

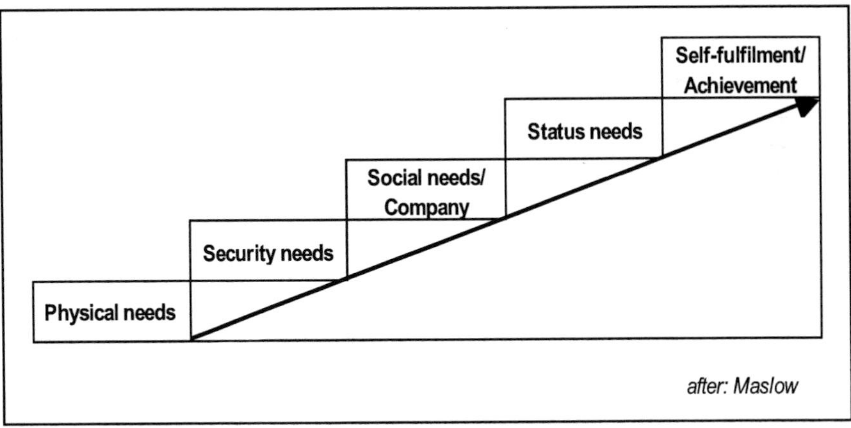

after: Maslow

As can be seen, the financial aspects of employment cover direct costs of living – hopefully meeting the needs of physical survival (food, drink etc) and Security needs (living accommodation) – but staff are also motivated by the atmosphere of teamwork and company at work. For some people, the aspiration of owning a prestige motor car or designer clothes may also provide considerable motivation but, if and when these are achieved, a new target tends to take their place.

Maslow argued that real fulfilment comes from:

- the longer-term achievement of commercial (and lifetime) targets and goals,
- the recognition which usually goes with this, and
- the feeling of personal growth as job demands change and grow – and if the individual's development matches this trend.

Of course, these 'higher motivators' only work if the earlier motivators are already met.

The manager, can have quite an influence upon the application of motivation methods to the team but, for full effect, the business needs to be at least matching the current 'going rates' for remuneration and benefits!

6. Applying the motivators

The modern agenda for managers, who are seeking to achieve high performing sales teams, are now working towards the following items:

Encouraging an obsession for customers

This includes developing an atmosphere of sharing the 'celebrations' of satisfied customers around the whole team – encouraging all team members to 'pool' their success stories and, equally, encouraging customers to share in the successes of the team (by inviting them to special events – wine and cheese promotions etc.).

These methods become much easier when the business has built up a database of regular and/or account customers.

Listening to customers

Regular customers often display a kind of 'fond ownership' of your business and have been known to provide quite a lot of feedback about this Season's ranges, what they liked about last year's offer – and the 'look' they prefer and may be looking for, for the next Season.

Businesses with 'local buyers' have a significant advantage over centrally bought businesses if customers' needs, preferences and interests are heeded.

Larger, 'centrally bought' businesses, have to use different methods of predicting consumer demand and identifying preferences but local teams do have a role in providing local feedback to the buying team.

Leading by example

Managers need to be able to lead as well as co-ordinate the efforts of the team. This means being able to do all the things that are asked of the sales team and doing them from time to time – not all the time! (See also Chapter 2).

Giving reward and recognition

Managers are free to generate their own team 'award' scheme – even though the 'benefits' may be non-monetary. For example, a domestic team league table could be posted in the Staff Room with a variety of measures used to determine 'employee of the month'. This might need to be more than a simple sales graph – so that the 'winners' are not simply the most experienced staff members each month (some focus could be placed on, for example, related sales).

Managing teamworking

As we have seen, the concept and reality of strong teamwork benefits everyone – individuals are bonded into the group, group members help each other, and when one member has a good day the whole team celebrates for them. None of this happens by accident or without serious effort by the leader; there are enough pressures in most average groups for the negative, destructive forces to threaten the stability and cohesion of any team. It takes a special person to make the team have a life of its own – as most of us know when we have worked with a successful sales team leader. These are essential skills for the future.

Encouraging career development opportunities

Good sales team leaders are prepared to acknowledge that the team is unlikely to hold top performers for ever and that some will be sufficiently ambitious to want to try out their abilities in running their own team somewhere else. Their contribution may be continued longer (and at a higher level) if the manager is able to offer coaching (alongside other career development opportunities such as open learning or Higher Education courses) so that, when the time comes to 'fly the nest', the ambitious leaver is well prepared to be successful in the new role. What better advertisement could there be for working in a successful business, for an effective sales team leader, and in a well motivated sales team (which is dedicated to the concepts and realities of high profile excellence in customer service and care)?

More tangible rewards – which can be extremely effective in the short-term – and avoid the 'cash label' include:

- **praise** – direct, customer compliments circulated, direct from the boss
- **recognition** – from peers, through a certificate or award, award dinner, press release
- **social functions** – sport/outdoor function, theatre tickets,
- **'extras'** – more training, more responsibilities, giving up lower level responsibilities
- **'status' factors** – e.g. car parking space, new tools (computer?), merchandise.

Assignment: Case Studies

The following examples illustrate how firms and front-line staff may 'take advantage' of customers. In each case, managers would certainly deny any personal encouragement or collaboration in the 'errors'. However, which reader has not heard of, or suspected, similar actions in their own past experiences – perhaps in other businesses?

Case Study 1: The wrong size

A shirt salesman was relieved to sell a shirt to an International businessman visiting London. This was a 'disaster' purchase – the customer desperately needed a new shirt – and was leaving London by the next flight to the USA. Subsequent discussion within the team revealed that the salesman had sold the customer the 'nearest size' as the customer's preferred style was out of stock in the right size. 'By the time he finds out, he'll be in Florida' the salesman was heard to say.

Points for discussion:

Why should a normally honest person behave in such a way?

What action would you take as the team leader?

Case Study 2: The more expensive option

A customer visited a store intending to place an order for a new kitchen – including a new oven. Her preferred choice for the oven was priced at £299 and she wished to check that this version, shown in the firm's catalogue, was still available. The sales assistant denied its very existence – claiming that only a 'look-alike' oven at £499 was now sold at the branch. 'I've never seen it', he said. The customer – confused and quite disappointed – then stated her original intention to order a new kitchen with the oven; this immediately brought a total change of attitude from the salesman – 'I'll check with the manager if we can order your oven, specially', he said. Returning from the manager with a broad smile, 5 minutes later, he was delighted to take the full order including the customer's preferred oven. When the ultimate delivery was made, the customer received the substitute oven, with no explanation.

Points for discussion:

Why did the salesman deny all knowledge of the first oven even though it was illustrated in the company's own current catalogue?

What brought about his sudden change of attitude?

How would you have felt if you had been the customer?

What action would you take as the leader?

Case Study 3: The hotel swimming pool

Holidaymakers are frequently warned in television holiday programmes to beware of booking holidays at hotels in brochures which are simply 'artists' impressions'. But things can go wrong in traditional hotels too. Who has experienced the Courier's casual warning about some facility which is out of service through some extenuating circumstance – yet the facility itself was a vital contributory reason for placing the booking in the first place? 'Just one thing I should tell you before we get to the Resort, unfortunately the swimming pool is out of service as a very bad storm at the weekend washed a lot of mud and sand into it'. What was not said was that the hotel staff/management had been looking at the mess for 4 or 5 days already, with no obvious sign of any corrective action. (cont)

Case Study 3 - (cont)

<u>Points for discussion:</u>

What action would you take if you were the customer (family of four including two children)?

What should the Representative have done?

If you were the Hotel Manager what would be your first priority?

8. Summary

We have seen in this chapter that good and consistent customer service does not just happen by accident – it requires:

- an appropriate culture adopted by the business as a whole
- enthusiastic team leaders with a missionary zeal for the importance of good service standards
- well motivated team members who are pleased to help each other to help customers and who are keen to develop and maintain a reputation for service excellence.

Later chapters in this section provide more detailed ways in which this process can be encouraged and enhanced.

Summary of Key Learning Points

1. Despite frequent denials and disbelief, most managers would agree that they have heard their front-line staff speak to customers in ways that caused their toes to 'curl up'.

2. Managers set the tone of the organisation when it comes to service standards – and they can become really good at that when they know that its results are measured and appreciated by their bosses.

3. There is no point in having a 'no fuss' refund policy if, when the customer takes up her right to it, she finds that the staff either resent/disbelieve her story or they are simply incompetent and cannot carry out the policy.

4. Thinly disguised contempt (TDC) should be replaced with explicitly proud delight (EPD) that customers use our business.

5. Managers play an important part in helping to keep customer service standards high.

6. Successful customer service staff quickly develop the skill of self-reflection – the ability to recognise their own strengths and weaknesses – and work on the improvement points themselves. Good managers encourage and assist with this process.

7. Positive attitudes are affected in staff by the levels of motivation which has been encouraged from the organisation in general, and the manager in particular.

Summary of Key Learning Points

8. **If you want people to apply a new system or approach, first encourage them to help invent it; ownership comes from involvement.**

9. **Whichever approach to motivation and reward is adopted, the atmosphere and culture of the business will have been affected in a major way.**

10. **It should always be remembered that, whilst money is a most important motivator, it is not the only one.**

11. **The manager can have quite an influence upon the application of motivation methods to the team but, for full effect, the business needs to be at least matching the current 'going rates' in the area for remuneration and benefits.**

7

Customer Care

What is it? And what is 'new' about it?

1. Introduction

Customer care – at its most literal – means ensuring that customers receive truly excellent service from the moment they set foot in your business (or make contact with your telephone switchboard operator) to the moment their purchases are home and in use. It all sounds common sense but, as with so many other things in life, it is less easy than it first appears. This is because of the things which conspire against us in meeting customer expectations. For example:

- ensuring the 'promise' made in the advertisement, window, fascia etc is 'matched' inside the business,
- providing a quality of fixturing/racking/furniture/design which enhances the presentation of the product or service,
- selecting merchandise which 'matches' the promoted price/image level of the business,
- adopting the management 'climate' which ensures that appropriate people are appointed to customer contact who are then trained and motivated to 'want' to perform to the best of their ability.

It may come as a surprise to some readers to find 'non-people' issues included in this list but when you think about it carefully our satisfaction with purchases begins with the availability of what we want to buy. It really does not matter if the product is the finest in the country (or even the world!) – if it is not available when and where you wish to buy it, no amount of 'soft talk' will satisfy you.

Customer satisfaction starts with ensuring availability of the things (or services) which customers wish to buy!

Obvious, you may say, but it is surprising how many businesses seem quite unable to maintain basic demand lines in stock and, more importantly train their staff to be able to 'switch sell' customers to alternative lines when the first product has sold-out.

What does the firm's 'image' have to do with it, either? Well, the customer can be persuaded to pay Rolls Royce prices if everything about the business matches the image of the car – this means quality advertising leaflets (on quality art-paper), quality decor in the showroom and stylish after-sales service. It is possible to buy quality cars from second-hand car dealers who occupy temporary accommodation, but the business will almost certainly not be exploiting its quality position if the office is in a garden shed – and no after-sales service is available!

Both these aspects may require significant investment – which you may have noticed your competitors undertaking – but the last point on the list requires much less money – only the application of standards and time.

This section is about managing customer care and much emphasis will be placed on the managing part. There is no doubt that caring for customers is everyone's responsibility in the business – but it is also a key performance area for every manager; not to do it – but certainly to see that it is done.

Setting standards for customer care – and then seeing that they are attained – is the responsibility of every manager! (This obviously includes internal customers as well as the external ones.)

2. What is 'new' about customer care?

In short – nothing! But why publish this book – and all the others, not to mention courses, films and so on? Business has become more and more competitive in recent years, fuelled no doubt by economic pressures – two serious recessions in a decade – and the entry into many markets of new businesses with much more aggressive marketing policies. To the traditional and long-established business this may seem 'unfair' and represent guerrilla tactics in your own backyard.

Fair or not, it represents reality for many business people and in some sectors has clearly produced much better choice of products, pricing and service to customers. Where this has not created more business in total, customers have found themselves testing out alternative suppliers with a consequent reduction in their loyalty to the more 'traditional' ones. Hasn't your business considered applying this process to your suppliers – especially those whose product/price/service mix appears to be increasingly uncompetitive?

The retail market has always been customer orientated – the whole process of buying and selling has no purpose without customers, and ignoring customer needs is a sure-fire way of treading the path towards business failure – and bankruptcy!

We can all bring to mind businesses which have failed – and some may have been pretty close to us (in our own High Street or precinct). Reasons often vary considerably, but a truly unforgivable cause is customer dissatisfaction. We should all have this aspect of our business under total control.

We are all human (as are all our colleagues, staff, bosses) – mistakes, 'off-days', losses of concentration do happen. Sometimes the results are catastrophic – and, if unchecked, can contribute to the decline and even the eventual demise of the business!

Case History

In one of the country's major tourist cities, there is a wide variety of fast-food 'takeaways'. The market is exceptionally competitive and the product on offer is wide – serving the tastes of a wide range of nationalities. A recent visit to one of these establishments was obviously on the 'wrong' day!

The assistant was glowering at everyone and the Chef/Manager appeared to be taking out his ill-humour on all the catering equipment. Customer service could only be described as 'surly'. Sitting within hearing distance of the counter, the customer could not fail to hear the following conversation between a regular customer and the Manager (probably also within earshot of the assistant herself):

Customer: 'I see Mabel is in her usual good mood!'

Manager: 'Yes, I don't know what gets into her!' (cont)

Case history (cont)

From this exchange, we can deduce several things:

- The staff member is regularly in a bad mood and doesn't care if it shows!
- The manager doesn't appear to care and seems to have 'given up' – siding with the customers against his employee.
- The way is wide open for the entrance of a new 'player' to 'steal' the business with comparable quality food and cheerful, polite and quality service.
- Who will the owner blame for the loss of business?

Unfortunately scenes like this are all too common in service-oriented businesses and, apart from addressing the staff member's causes of the bad moods, the failure invariably lies with management!

3. The 'customer's revenge'

In today's market, customers are being encouraged to seek out quality services from all kinds of services organisations in society. For example:

- doctors, dentists, hospitals, etc.
- transport services
- fuel suppliers.

Many of these are operating 'Charter' schemes through which dissatisfied customers are being positively encouraged to complain and, if a review of their complaint proves that they have been let down, they are actually rewarded. This may not ring true to some readers, but the truth is that most Britons are much too tolerant of poor service and failures to meet customer expectations. These schemes have already had quite an effect on many customers – and may just have caused people to be more demanding of their suppliers.

Against this backcloth, market leaders have reinforced their customer service policies – matching, for example, the unqualified exchange/refund policies of Argos and the price promise of the John Lewis Partnership. Many other specialist (and sometimes quite small) businesses have followed suit and this has also contributed to greater competitive pressure being applied to less marketing-conscious businesses.

So, if some customers seem to have become more demanding, it should be no surprise. Crude statistics are often quoted (and misquoted!) about customer satisfaction and dissatisfaction, but the following quotation has stood the real test of time …

Case Histories

Nobody really knows the exact cost of a disgruntled customer, but it is high. The Ford Motor Company carried out a Market Research study which showed that a happy customer tells, on average, 8 people the good news about the product; a dissatisfied customer tells, on average, more than 20 people. (This quotation reveals much higher figures than those which are often quoted in public seminars.)

Anita Roddick, founder of the Body Shop group, makes much of the 'vigilante customer' and the power they have for discriminating against any non-ethical behaviour in companies or their suppliers. However this may be difficult to predict and still more difficult to control. The problem is that, once the Press have exposed some trading 'difficulty' it may be very difficult to counter any negative effects – even if the story is actually incorrect.

Here is the nub of the problem, dissatisfied customers may be unseen, unrecorded, unmeasured – but they have the capacity to work directly against the organisation's advertising and marketing efforts!

4. The big picture

To understand the integrated nature of the whole customer care topic, we have prepared the flow-chart diagram opposite:

This flow-chart enables us to appreciate:

- the importance of each part to the whole picture
- that customer service may be the piece of the 'jigsaw' which sometimes goes 'wrong', but the real cause may lie elsewhere
- how easily that overall market image may be dented by a 'failure' in one very small cell.

Assignment

Taking two 'highlighters' (or coloured pencils):

- colour in all those squares for which you, as a manager, have full responsibility, then
- colour in (different colour) those for which you have partial responsibility.

You may be surprised by just how much falls within your responsibility area and how much influence you have in this vital area of the business!

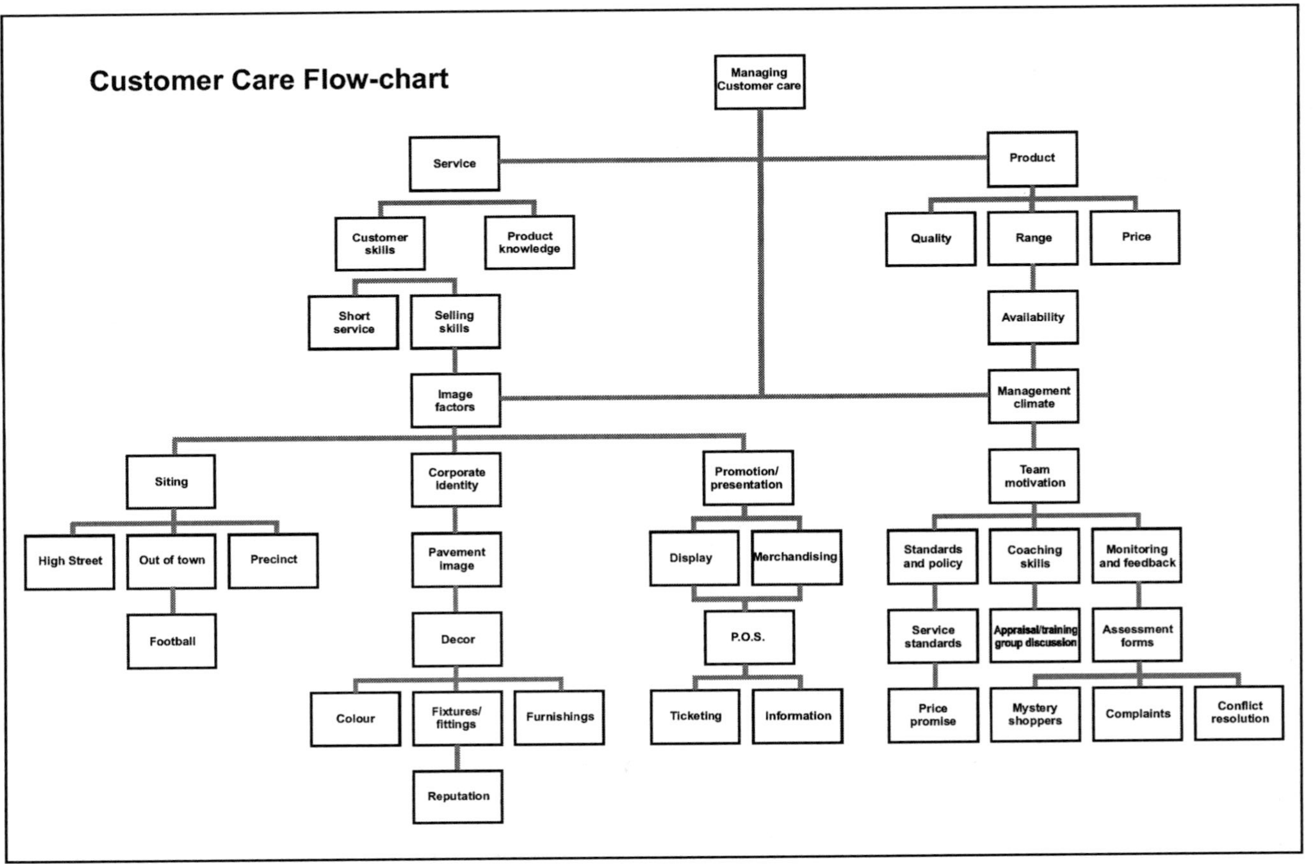
Customer Care Flow-chart
Managing Customer care
Service
Product
Customer skills
Product knowledge
Quality
Range
Price
Short service
Selling skills
Availability
Image factors
Management climate
Siting
Corporate identity
Promotion/ presentation
Team motivation
High Street
Out of town
Precinct
Pavement image
Display
Merchandising
Standards and policy
Coaching skills
Monitoring and feedback
Football
Decor
P.O.S.
Service standards
Appraisal/training group discussion
Assessment forms
Colour
Fixtures/ fittings
Furnishings
Ticketing
Information
Price promise
Mystery shoppers
Complaints
Conflict resolution
Reputation

5. Management challenge

So, the reader should have no doubt that re-examining managers' roles in enhancing and maintaining customer care standards in the business is very definitely your responsibility! Following the advice in this book will help with this whole process.

However, before we address these issues in more depth, we should consider what has stopped this being done as a natural part of business. The following barriers need careful thought before rushing into a new initiative – for lasting results, they will need to be addressed and tackled as an integral part of your development plan. Typical barriers are:

- **Complacency** – *'We have been in business for 'n' years – what do we need all this for now? If customers had a complaint, they would tell us ... my time is taken up with this advertising campaign/trying to attract more business!'*
- **'It's not my job'** – *'If the MD/boss thought all this was needed he/she would say so. We don't go in for these new-fangled things/American ideas here!'*
- **Attack** – *'I've called a staff meeting and I'm going to have a good go at them! The trouble is, they don't really listen. All people are interested in today is money and no one really cares about the customer any more.'*
- **Secret shoppers** – *'We attended this meeting at HQ and this dude they called the Marketing Controller came in and gave us a right ... ticking off about our customer service. Do you know what they did? They sent the spies/KGB into the branches and gave us a right wigging about the reports. If you ask me, firms that do that kind of thing aren't worth working for!'*
- **Old ideas** – *'My boss says he remembers some kind of customer 'initiative' in the 70s and it didn't work then. These schemes are just invented to keep the backroom boys in a job!'*
- **Real priorities** – *'I'll give more attention to customer care when I've got the hang of this new computer system they've given us to learn. This firm is really only interested in the paperwork. If that's neat, tidy and accurate they keep off your back. Customers? We don't have enough time to devote to them!'*

Hopefully not too many readers will have said any of these things, but quite a few must have heard them from time to time. The trouble is that, while the underlying attitudes are clearly wrong and unhelpful, there may just be a grain of truth in each statement. Furthermore, the fact that you have not actually heard these things doesn't mean that they are not talked about in the queue for the bus (after work) or in the staff room.

If things are to improve, relations between Manager and customer care staff have to be built on real honesty and trust or the effectiveness of the whole initiative will founder!

Assignment

Given the attitudes expressed in the above section, write your own responses to the speakers in each of the panels below:

'We have been in business for 'n' years – what do we need all this for now?'

____

____

'If customers had a complaint they would tell us .... my time is taken up with this advertising campaign/trying to attract more business!'

____

____

'If the MD/boss thought all this was needed he/she would say so.'

____

____

'We don't go in for these new–fangled things/American ideas here!'

____

____

'I've called a staff meeting and I'm going to have a good go at them!'

____

____

'The trouble is they don't really listen. All people are interested in today is money and no one really cares about the customer any more!'

____

____

'We attended this meeting at HQ and this bloke they called the Marketing Controller came in and gave us a right ...... ticking off about our customer service.'

'Do you know what they did, they sent the spies/KGB into the branches and gave us a right wigging about the reports. If you ask me, firms that do that kind of thing aren't worth working for!'

'My Boss says he remembers some kind of customer 'initiative' in the 70's and it didn't work then.'

'These schemes are just invented to keep the backroom boys in a job!'

'I'll give more attention to customer care when I've got the hang of this new computer system they've given us to learn.'

'This firm is really only interested in the paperwork. If that's neat, tidy and accurate they keep off your back. Customers? We don't have enough time to devote to them!'

6. Summary

This chapter has sought to establish the fundamental principles of:

- Why customer care programmes are important
- How unsatisfied customers can undo all your good marketing efforts
- What kind of attitudes are prevalent in this field , and why ... and lastly,

- What attitude the manager should take towards the cynics and the lazy.

Customers provide the lifeblood of our businesses; they are not incidental but must be the main purpose of them. We must attract, nurture and delight them or they may be tempted away by our competitors!

Summary of Key Learning Points

1. **Customer satisfaction starts with ensuring availability of the products or services which customers wish to buy.**

2. **Setting standards for customer care – and then seeing that they are attained – is the responsibility of every manager. (This obviously includes internal customers as well as the external ones).**

3. **We are all human – as are all our colleagues, staff, bosses etc. Mistakes, 'off-days', losses of concentration do happen. Sometimes the results are catastrophic – and, if unchecked, can contribute to the decline and even the eventual demise of the business!**

4. **Unfortunately scenes involving poor service are all too common in some businesses and, apart from addressing the staff member's causes of bad moods, the failure lies with management.**

5. **Dissatisfied customers may be unseen, unrecorded, unmeasured but they have the capacity to work directly against the organisation's advertising and marketing efforts.**

6. **If things are to improve, relations between manager and customer care staff have to be built on real honesty and trust or the effectiveness of the whole initiative will founder.**

7. **Customers provide the lifeblood of our businesses; they are not incidental but must be the main purpose of them. We must attract, nurture and delight them or they may be tempted away by our competitors.**

8

The 'Upside-Down' Organisation

Modern approaches for high performance

1. Introduction

Do you remember the days when we had to form separate queues in the Bank or Post Office and arrived at the front just in time for the cashier to put up the 'Closed' sign? Or perhaps demanding to see a Hotel Manager to present a complaint and being shown to a back office completely screened from the rest of the world – and especially from the 'front desk', where the real customers are?

In many large businesses today, the private offices have gone, and have been replaced by open-plan offices, glass panelled 'horse-boxes' or, perhaps, no offices at all for the people responsible for 'the show'... Why should 'blue chip' organisations have placed their own managers under what might feel like pressure or attack?

It has been said that the easiest way to take your eye off the ball is to ignore its very presence! It may be easy for some people to ignore customers – especially the 'difficult' ones who are 'best left to others anyway' – if they cannot be seen; and, more to the point, if the customer is unable to see the manager.

This should not be taken as a debate about the importance of having a quiet place to work – for confidentiality in private meetings – or for the best facilities for handling paperwork in a systematic way. Quiet offices are needed – but can be shared or borrowed.

What customers clearly appreciate is being able to see and access a manager – a person who is ultimately responsible for the smooth-running of the operation – and who can be witnessed actually going about his or her business of managing. How many times have you stood on a railway platform or concourse to be informed over the tannoy that trains are cancelled or delayed – with no one to speak to (face-to-face) about your particular travelling problem?

True customer-facing organisations ensure that there are managers accessible by, and to, customers – and that they are trained to cope with the related difficulties – emotion, aggression, rudeness and naked anger!

So, how does this square with the idea of delegation, empowerment and even de-layering inside organisations? In this chapter, we will examine the case for removing managers' offices and putting all the managers out onto the sales floor.

2. Whose business is it, really?

We can easily confuse ownership with belonging. We all know – and that includes the customer, of course – that the business is owned by someone. They also know that the owner might be the latest generation representative of a long established family – or a horde of institutional shareholders acting on behalf of expectant pensioners. Ultimately, though, real 'influence' at the sharp-end lies with the manager – even though the higher you go, the more power may be exercised. (This explains why so many angry customers send their complaints direct to the Managing Director rather than seeking redress from the local manager). However, we should re-address the question of ownership and look at it through the eyes of regular customers.

In society today, many people feel a frustrated sense of ownership for their town, their street, their library and even their local favourite shops. They can sometimes be heard saying: 'What have they done to *our store*?', while changes may be the source of some complaint as well as congratulations.

Here, we could debate many peoples' attitudes towards change – their resistance to it, and often, their exclusion from it. But businesses have to move on – progress – and need to avoid upsetting existing customers, at the same time re-orientating themselves towards attracting new ones.

'What have they done to our store?' expresses a degree of public ownership far beyond the actuality of shareholding. Is this really wrong? Surely this must be just about one of the most flattering statements of customer loyalty we are ever likely to hear? Perhaps we are really just custodians for the business which belongs to our customers and we are here to facilitate their patronage of it?

Case History

During a management seminar presented for branch managers of a multiple retailer, the question of how to handle customer complaints was raised. In the following discussion, one manager accused another of dishonesty, which created some considerable controversy.

It transpired that, when a customer demanded to see 'Mr Scroggs' (the family name on the fascia board) the Manager greeted the customer and never gave his own name – leaving the customer with the impression that he was the owner.

Did this matter? Did customers feel any better when they thought they were being dealt with by the firm's owner? Possibly!

No serious damage could come from this 'impersonation' – but the example gives an interesting insight into Customers' preparedness to believe that the Manager of their store is, in fact, 'Mr Big'!

So, is there a distinction between ownership and belonging?

If we have targeted our customer profile correctly, then those people will feel a sense of belonging – comfort – in our shop or store and, just like close friends, they will prefer to visit us when they come to choose their purchases!

Can we say the same for ourselves and our teams?

3. The customer is 'King'- but who is the boss?

One of the arts of good people management is to encourage employees to feel a sense of belonging in the business – not to restrain it or to fix it in time – but to make it progressive and even more successful. Even so, this feeling cannot overtake the reality that the whole show is provided solely to benefit the customers and all sales staff should help encourage this feeling too.

But this is not the feeling we obtain when we visit some businesses. Far from the staff wanting to share their success with customers, they focus mainly on their own problems and interests and, sometimes, even exude a kind of 'protectionism' for the stock (rather like a pet shop owner wanting to ensure his/her favourite rabbit goes to a good home). So, how should it be?

In the 'topsy-turvy' organisation the 'Customer is King' and the key personnel, from the customer's viewpoint, are the front-line staff. All the rest of us are support staff.

The 'Customer is King' statement may be a cliché; surely you have heard it before – but does it really work that way in your organisation?

Case History

One of the largest, world class companies in the computer industry took its "eye off the ball". Customers were leaving and moving to competitors and the business was in decline. After a serious review, the business adopted a "customer-facing organisation" chart which emphasised a mega-shift of style. Dramatically, the President (or Managing Director) was placed at the bottom of the organisation chart diagram with the whole management team providing support to all the customer-facing staff, who were placed at the top of the tree. This single step led to the gradual renaissance of IBM.

The following revision to our flow-chart illustrates this point graphically. The most important 'support person' is the Managing Director, and the most important people – to customers – are the front-line staff.

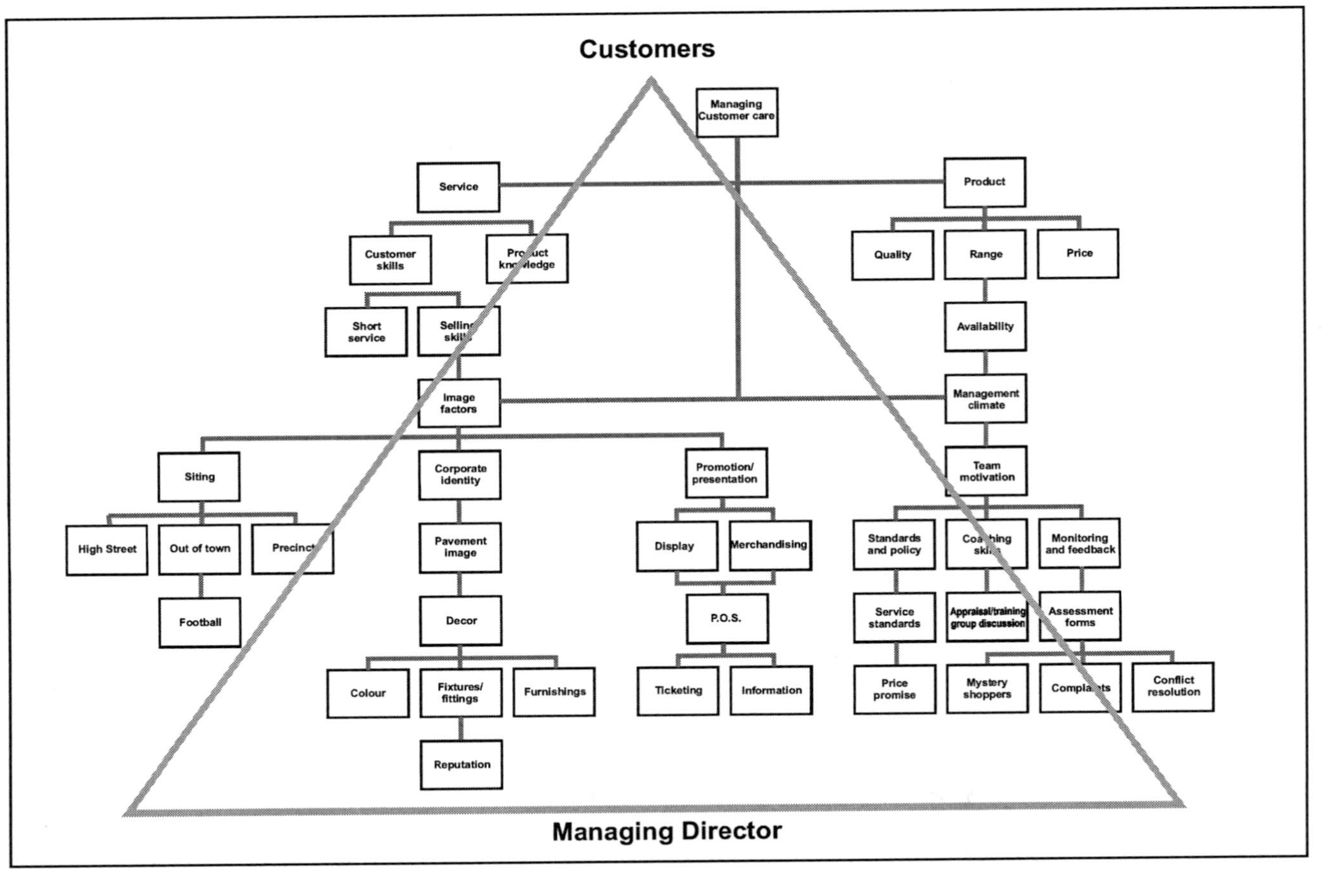
Customers
Managing Customer care
Service
Product
Customer skills
Product knowledge
Quality
Range
Price
Short service
Selling skills
Availability
Image factors
Management climate
Siting
Corporate identity
Promotion/ presentation
Team motivation
High Street
Out of town
Precinct
Pavement image
Display
Merchandising
Standards and policy
Coaching skills
Monitoring and feedback
Football
Decor
P.O.S.
Service standards
Appraisal/training group discussion
Assessment forms
Colour
Fixtures/ fittings
Furnishings
Ticketing
Information
Price promise
Mystery shoppers
Complaints
Conflict resolution
Reputation
Managing Director

If they are:

- well trained, highly skilled and knowledgeable
- secure,
- motivated and happy,
- ambitious for the business,

...it will really show. And do their managers, and the specialists in the business, facilitate this success or do they hinder it? If you are not sure about the accuracy of your answers to these questions, try out the following assignment with your team members (but do it informally, please!).

Assignment: Perceptions of Team Members

1 How well does the team feel they are supported with training in:

a) Selling Skills b) Service Standards c) Handling 'difficult' people d) Product Features/ Benefits e) Selling Systems?

At:

Advanced Refresher or Basic levels?

Would they describe such support as:

i) Excellent ii) Some gaps - patchy iii) Inadequate?

2 How much leadership support do they feel they receive - from:

a) Top management b) Company specialists c) Immediate Manager?

Is access to each of these levels:

i) Adequate ii) Inadequate (some details would be welcome!)

3 How secure do team members feel:

a) In their job b) In the Company c) In their lives?

i) Very secure ii) Adequately secure iii) Quite insecure?

4 How well-motivated would individual team members be, to work outside normal hours without pay or complaint :(i.e. only reward is Manager's recognition and thanks)?

a In emergency only b Occasionally c Regularly?

5 To what extent would this example reflect individuals/ motivation in other situations?

a) Always b) Occasionally c) Not at all

6 How ambitious are individual team members for the success of the business?

a) Very ambitious (e.g. propose ideas and suggestions regularly)
b) Will respond if prompted or c) Rarely give thought or suggestion

4. The case for empowerment

The whole point of organisations is that each job level should be discrete from the previous one – the skills are different but build on those learned before. This is how organisational structure works.

The further the job is from the customer, the greater the risk that the person holding the job loses 'touch' with the whole idea of customer needs!

The other problem with the traditional approach is that some line managers become tempted to take over the roles of their team members rather than to enable them to do them better. This becomes a lot worse when the managers themselves are struggling with their responsibilities and targets.

One 'solution' to this is to ensure that a new agenda of training is formed, as we will consider at the end of this chapter.

Case History – The faulty lightbulb

One of the UK's famous variety chain stores sells light bulbs. A customer bought a pair of 60w bulbs and fitted one to a table lamp on return home. The new bulb immediately 'blew' and so the customer took the bulb back to the store on the same day. She took the bulb to the 'Service Desk' at the rear of the store but was re-directed to the checkout at the front of the store. At the checkout, the operator had to complete a 'refund form' – and then call a Supervisor, who had to drop what she was doing on the rear Service Desk and come and countersign the form. The operator was then able to open the till and give 78p back to the customer. By this time a long queue of customers had formed at the checkout!

Security rules on cash are important but is it not possible to trust and empower staff to refund up to, say, £2 without having to call a Supervisor? The process would still be subjected to random checks and would enable the Supervisor to concentrate on his or her own job.

Such changes can only be possible when both parties trust each other and training and coaching are provided on a constant basis.

The truth is that quality service can be achieved from a well trained and motivated workforce and, when these factors are met, additional benefits are usually gained!

- a reduction in selling errors (e.g. wrong size sold, wrong change given, errors in paperwork become the exception – not the rule.)
- complaints are infrequent
- customers actually enjoy their visit and plan their return visits (and may even tell the firm so!) .... and,
- front-line staff begin to 'think ahead' for their managers (i.e. they begin to think like managers.).

Case History

Most fashion retailers provide an alterations service as part of their customer service policy. Some make charges for this service – others do not.

The Flannels Group, leading fashion retailer based in the North West, empowers staff to decide if and when charges might be appropriate.

During a coaching session with a new staff member, a Team Manager was asked by a customer if the firm could alter a pair of trousers (bought from another shop). The Manager had noticed how interested the customer had seemed to be in the merchandise displays and stated that there would be no charge. The customer was most impressed – even more so by the speed of the service – and the new staff member took down the instructions immediately for a delivery time of 2 hours! The customer was so impressed that he went on to buy a fashion suit for over £700.

Of course, none of this happens without a great deal of hard work. A consequence of recognising the true importance of customers and service to them, is the need to ensure:

- realistic service standards are defined and set for staff to meet
- the provision of high quality training to ensure that front-line staff are able to provide really expert service (to meet those standards)

The reality is that many businesses fail to give adequate leadership or the necessary resources to achieve realistic service standards and provision of high quality service training!

So, what needs to be done?

The starting point is to set out a new agenda for management training – as we can see in the next section.

5. The new management agenda

In today's market, employers are asking for managers who can:

- work comfortably with people of all kinds of character, nationality and upbringing and who are able to build trust for, and within, the team
- communicate clearly, persuasively, eloquently – as a teacher or mentor as much as the team leader
- make decisions with self-confidence – and with help
- embrace and work with change – with resourcefulness and adaptability
- lead, delegate, listen to the team – and be able to reward good performance appropriately.

These are the factors which are now distancing the 'market leaders' in most markets from the 'also-rans'. Which one do you want to be?

Assignment

This chapter has sought to set out an agenda for change. To begin to work towards new Customer Care standards, ask yourself:

1 What action do I need to take to be more supportive of my front-line staff?

2 Am I sufficiently accessible to them (all)?

3 When I am accessible, do I invariably:

- show trust in them?
- make the necessary decision?
- show that I embrace and work with change?
- listen sympathetically and communicate persuasively?
- teach and train?
- lead and delegate when this is appropriate?
- recognise and reward good performance in an appropriate way?

(cont)

Assignment (cont)

Make notes. If you are uncertain about your answers to these questions, perhaps you could obtain some additional feedback from other colleagues who know you well? Now would also be a good time to commit yourself to an action plan to "improve/overcome" any gaps which this questionnaire might have revealed.

And, finally, if your organisation has already tried to implement these ideas and you feel that they are not working sufficiently well, you might benefit from reviewing this chapter again – with a view to considering whether this lack of success was because of:

- insufficient commitment from:

  a) your team?
  b) you?
  c) senior management?

- insufficient resources made available for:

  d) training?
  e) rewards?

What could be done to breathe new life into the approach?

6. Summary

This chapter has sought to set out an agenda for change. Any manager can influence change within his or her own team as well as others in the organisation, although this is much more likely to happen when positive encouragement is given (by senior management) to create positive results in customer service and care.

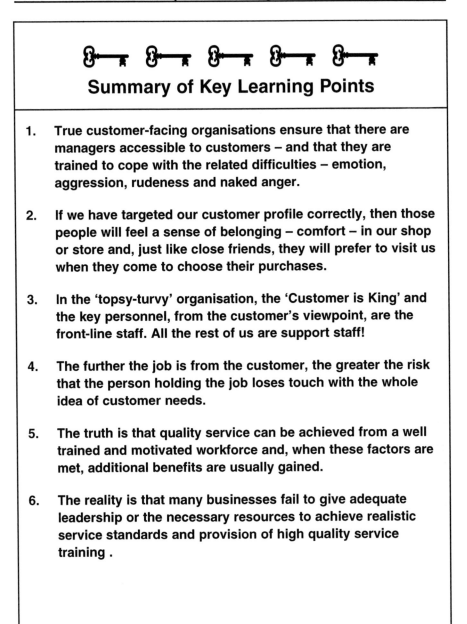

Summary of Key Learning Points

1. **True customer-facing organisations ensure that there are managers accessible to customers – and that they are trained to cope with the related difficulties – emotion, aggression, rudeness and naked anger.**

2. **If we have targeted our customer profile correctly, then those people will feel a sense of belonging – comfort – in our shop or store and, just like close friends, they will prefer to visit us when they come to choose their purchases.**

3. **In the 'topsy-turvy' organisation, the 'Customer is King' and the key personnel, from the customer's viewpoint, are the front-line staff. All the rest of us are support staff!**

4. **The further the job is from the customer, the greater the risk that the person holding the job loses touch with the whole idea of customer needs.**

5. **The truth is that quality service can be achieved from a well trained and motivated workforce and, when these factors are met, additional benefits are usually gained.**

6. **The reality is that many businesses fail to give adequate leadership or the necessary resources to achieve realistic service standards and provision of high quality service training .**

9

Mission and Vision-Building

A new agenda for managers

1. Introduction

Every organisation has a purpose, or it would not exist! The reality is that many organisations have forgotten what that purpose is – or, more to the point, they have lost their way. For example, making a profit is a perfectly satisfactory goal but it may not be easily achieved without a clear strategy which embraces the customers whose patronage enable that profit to be made.

This chapter provides a 'workshop approach' to help managers re-define their own approach to their business, and consider how well their teams reflect this.

2. Purpose notes

The purpose of a convenience store could be described as:

- to offer a range of goods for sale which customers
  - require on a frequent basis
  - often need at 'unsocial hours'
- to make a profit.

It does not take much imagination to create an image of a corner store in a suburb or village which is open all hours and stocks all the basic demand items that local customers may suddenly discover they need in the middle of cooking or preparing a meal and will visit the local business because it saves on the bus fare or petrol against the visit to the out-of-town superstore.

So, what is the purpose of ***your*** firm? Perhaps to clarify these thoughts in your mind you should make some notes here:

Purpose notes

This task may not have seemed particularly demanding but it is an essential step before deciding on a Mission Statement for the organisation.

3. Mission statement

What is the point of a mission statement?

All that the mission statement does is to provide a uniting, central statement around which the whole of the firm's people can unite in its understanding of what is involved in meeting its purpose!

So, the corner shop might have described its mission statement thus:

> To provide a friendly, comfortable service – supplying all the basic needs required in typical households within walking distance of the shop – at the time when those needs arise – with emphasis on neighbourhood customer care, using customers' names wherever possible.
>
> The aim is for the friendliness of Budgens, coupled with the presentation

of Waitrose, the price promise of the Co-op and the credit facility of the local Public House.

The use of 'benchmark' named companies provides a clearer focus for the 'audience' for the mission statement (mostly the staff team). It should create understanding and commitment to what the company is trying to achieve.

Mission statements – on their own – will achieve little unless they are widely 'briefed into' the people in the organisation! Even then, the process needs to be converted from a statement of (almost!) the obvious and into a clear vision and activity goals for everyone to work towards!

Without these implementation stages, a mission statement may simply be a succession of dreams. This chapter seeks to demonstrate the importance of a Strategy for the formation of change in the customer care area and sets out a new agenda for management skills in support of the initiative. (A publicly promoted Mission Statement is included at the end of this chapter).

4. Developing a sense of vision

The following diagram gives an overview of the process, and of where visioning fits into the process of 'winning the hearts and minds' of your team members – who are the people who have to put it all into practice. Short-cuts in these areas will have little benefit – and may lead to half-hearted support for what may be seen as arbitrary customer service standards.

So, having a vision and being able to promote it to your team, helps to bridge the gap between the Mission Statement and what actually has to be done – and when.

It will also need to take account of that most favourite of marketing tools – known as the SWOT analysis (Strengths, Weaknesses, Opportunities and Threats).

Without vision, principles can lead to apoplexy and action may be haphazard!

Your vision will call for change and will help to answer the question:

> What will be different as a consequence of our work – later this year, next year, by the end of the decade?

When you are ready to brief your team – or refresh their commitment to the firm's mission – you might find yourself saying:

> For example, my vision is of customers leaving our store and being overheard to say: 'I always like coming in here, they are so friendly and helpful – nothing seems to be too much trouble and we always seem to find what we want.'

Of course, there are any number of businesses where the first part of this statement could be made, and even more where the second part could be said – but rather fewer where both elements are totally integrated. In larger businesses, it may be even more difficult to ensure consistency across all departments and locations. Whose responsibility is this? Simple answer – Management's responsibility!

The vision may have been inadequately 'sold' down the line or some local manager's found it difficult to identify with? Or, just as likely, the long-serving staff in the team cannot see any reason to change behaviour which has been acceptable over the years!

This is not a recipe for success!

Assignment: Your own vision statement

Now write a vision statement for customer care for your team.

Survey

A recent survey* of the UK's top Chief Executives revealed that they felt that most managers are better fitted for managing continuing "downturn" rather than a continuing economic upturn and that they are too preoccupied with cost-cutting. Specific skills they thought essential are: Leadership, Vision, People Management, Communications and Financial Literacy. Of these, 52% selected Vision as the weakest skill in most managers!

** Sunday Times*

5. Goals, priorities and action plans

The best visions have little value if the manager is unable to translate them into action. As we saw in Part One, managers need to be able to set priorities for their teams which coincide with the overall goals which have been set. It is not our purpose here to discuss all the distractions which may lead managers (and their teams) away from current work priorities – however, some managers do have difficulties in sorting out their action plans from all the different conflicting demands on their time. A simple device to overcome this is the 'How-To' decision chart. An example follows.

Decision Chart

The following chart illustrates how a goal may be achieved by following a decision-tree approach.

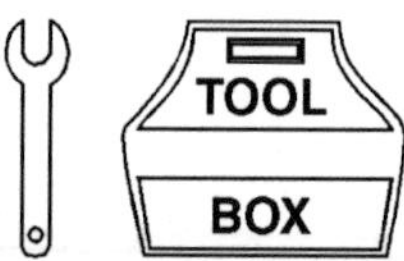

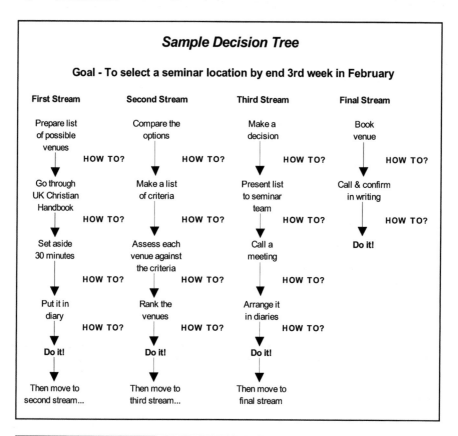

Sample Decision Tree

Goal - To select a seminar location by end 3rd week in February

First Stream	Second Stream	Third Stream	Final Stream
Prepare list of possible venues	Compare the options	Make a decision	Book venue
↓ HOW TO?	↓ HOW TO?	↓ HOW TO?	↓ HOW TO?
Go through UK Christian Handbook	Make a list of criteria	Present list to seminar team	Call & confirm in writing
↓ HOW TO?	↓ HOW TO?	↓ HOW TO?	↓ HOW TO?
Set aside 30 minutes	Assess each venue against the criteria	Call a meeting	**Do it!**
↓ HOW TO?	↓ HOW TO?	↓ HOW TO?	
Put it in diary	Rank the venues	Arrange it in diaries	
↓ HOW TO?	↓ HOW TO?	↓ HOW TO?	
Do it!	**Do it!**	**Do it!**	
↓	↓	↓	
Then move to second stream...	Then move to third stream...	Then move to final stream	

Assignment

Taking a current Goal (or objective), try to produce a decision tree which will enable the goal to be achieved. Then consider what distractions and barriers might need to be overcome if the objective is to be achieved.

6. The new management agenda (revisited)

As we have seen, the above foundation steps are fundamental if a new attempt at improving customer care is to work – and have lasting benefit. However, the 'new management agenda' is also critical if a new initiative is not to be seen by customers and staff alike, as a 'flash in the pan'.

In short, this agenda includes:

- **Focusing all attention and action on Customers**
  (in other words, if an action proposed does not 'pay-off' for customers, we don't do it!)
- **Reacting to ideas and suggestions from customers and staff**
  (this means not just listening but actually taking some action.)
- **Providing leadership**
  (ensuring that you set a good example and 'lead from the front')
- **Developing expertise in the team**
  (from this 'new' perspective, training is an essential – not a reward or a luxury.)
- **Encouraging creativity and contributions**
  (this means actively encouraging and nurturing the team until the ideas start flowing – and ensuring you listen and recognise them.)
- **Taking Risks**
  (this is likely to apply in the ways in which you try to use the resources of the business – a new staff rota, a new merchandise layout or display)
- **Counselling**
  (serving the needs of individual staff members by supporting them when they are in difficulties).

Before we now describe each of these activities in more detail, this could be an appropriate moment for you to complete the following assignment:

Assignment: Self-Audit

Here are those key functions again – rate yourself on the scale 1 to 5 (5 = high skills, while 1 = low skills). (This is likely to have greater accuracy if you are able to 'benchmark' yourself against another manager – maybe someone who has higher skills than yourself.)

1 Customer focus	**1**	**2**	**3**	**4**	**5**
2 Providing leadership	**1**	**2**	**3**	**4**	**5**
3 Developing the team's expertise	**1**	**2**	**3**	**4**	**5**
4 Encouraging creativity	**1**	**2**	**3**	**4**	**5**
5 Taking risks	**1**	**2**	**3**	**4**	**5**
6 Counselling	**1**	**2**	**3**	**4**	**5**

One interesting point about this list is that it already assumes full competence in the 'technical' dimensions of the manager's job – that is, product familiarity, accounting and financial skills. These are important, of course, (and described in some detail in Part 3 of this book) but they may not help the manager help his staff achieve a more productive relationship with customers.

Success in the technical dimensions of the manager's job may not help the staff achieve a more productive relationship with customers!

7. The manager's role

So, in this 'new world', what should the manager's role be?

Apart from those 'key functions' we listed above, managers have the tasks to manage:

- the purpose of the organisation
- the processes and performance
- the team members
- the culture of the business

...and each of these factors contributes significantly to the success of the organisation. Perhaps this all seems too familiar for it to be branded 'new';

the reader should perhaps reconsider these factors from the angle of their contribution to customer care.

8. Managing the purpose of the organisation

Clearly, this is a major priority for any manager – but we saw earlier that, in the case of IBM, many people lost sight of the purpose of the organisation with nearly disastrous results.

Every manager needs to have a clear understanding of the following issues and a work pattern which encourages others around him or her to support the Organisation Purpose!

We have already considered the first priority:

Having a clear vision and sense of mission

This assumes, firstly, that these have been devised for the organisation to unite behind and, secondly, that the manager has 'bought-into' the process.

Managers who are not committed themselves will find it difficult to gain the commitment of their team members!

Establishing objectives and standards

Someone has to be able to translate the philosophy and ideas of the organisation into understandable and meaningful action. You can almost imagine some members of your team thinking (if not actually verbalising): 'So what do you actually want us to do differently, Boss?' and the manager needs to have a convincing answer ready – not simply: 'We are doing it already' or, 'More of the same, really!'.

Such statements destroy any vision of improvement – 'crisper service', 'meeting customer's expectations' and 'creating customer delight' would be more appropriate!

Measuring customer satisfaction

At first sight this might seem difficult to do. However, it is possible if you can find ways of obtaining feedback from customers. This element would include complaints letters but 'customer satisfaction' should not be assumed just because of the absence of written complaints. Some businesses seek specific feedback from customers using feedback cards supplied around the business. (A competition could provide an incentive for them to be returned.)

Leading and managing change

It takes an enormous effort to be at least one jump ahead of one's competitors – and even more to stay ahead! Change of any kind will probably be viewed with a great deal of suspicion but ultimately standing still is no longer a desirable option.

Staff education and motivation

It is often forgotten just how these two apparently distinct and separate factors are, in fact, strongly connected. Education embraces, but does not replace, direct skills training – here it is deliberately focused on the individual's broader understanding of themselves (their strengths and weaknesses), the business (its aspirations and mission) and how they fit together in the wider world of the customers. Without doubt, a clear grasp of these roles and functions helps to create motivated people!

Case History – 'Good morning and good night'

A newly appointed manager in a non-selling department had been promoted from a position in which she had been able to recruit her own team. She had managed to generate considerable personal loyalty from her colleagues and there was a close bond between them. However, in the first few days with the new team, she was dismayed that individual team members in the 'general office' arrived and went home without even bothering to say 'good morning' or 'good night' to her. It was not that she expected them to express any Victorian-style subservience but just that it seemed to be an offensive denial of her very existence! Gentle pressure – and frequent presence in the general office at the start and end of the day – brought about gradual change but it took almost three months for her role to be accepted and a genuine welcome to be extended at the beginning of each day!

Points for consideration:

How might you have tackled the problem?

How might the team's lack of feeling affect relationships with 'customers'?

Team-building

The starting point for team building lies with the manager; and recognising that team working is actually a good thing. (Some managers misuse their power by creating such a competitive or 'divide-and-rule' atmosphere that any attempt at teamworking is 'suffocated at birth'). In fact, through poor people management skills, the only teamwork that is to be witnessed in some businesses is a 'negative unity' against the boss. (This may not be evidenced in outright rebellion – but certainly in 'feet-dragging'! Contrast this with the very apparent dynamism of a 'can-do, will-do' successful team.)

Some managers or bosses need assistance (and training) to help them achieve such a different climate in which performance may need holding back – not cajoled out of team members.

Listening to feedback

Most of us have been accused, at various times of hearing, but not listening!

A good Retail Manager is capable of listening – because most of us have been given two ears – but it may be that we do not use them nearly enough. And we can all use empathy and care to encourage team members to talk to us, but do we hear what is not said as well as what is said? Apart from this, do we take appropriate action based on what we hear?

Leading creativity and development

The dynamism which springs from the strong motivation and education mentioned above is likely to evaporate unless it is steered towards practical applications inside the business. Original ideas on selling skills and customer care may not be that easy to create – just keeping the team 'fresh' and enthusiastic can be a great achievement – but who says that training sessions should always be run by the manager, anyway? Often the team includes people who run Societies and Clubs in their spare time – why can't they be encouraged to play a leading part in a team meeting or training session? (Obviously the manager may need to provide help with this – but rotating the task may have an amazing effect!).

9. Summary

This image of your team as a thriving, highly enthusiastic group, coming up with lots of constructive ideas on how the business might be improved, may seem rather distant from current reality! Working on these factors takes time, and progress may be slow, with many setbacks on the road!

However, when progress is made, the reward in terms of:

- **team atmosphere and morale**
- **individual performance**
- **enthusiasm**
- **support, automatically provided between team members ...**

... can be really dramatic – to the extent team leaders may find themselves wondering how they ever managed before!

A clear recipe for achieving this vision is contained in the next three chapters.

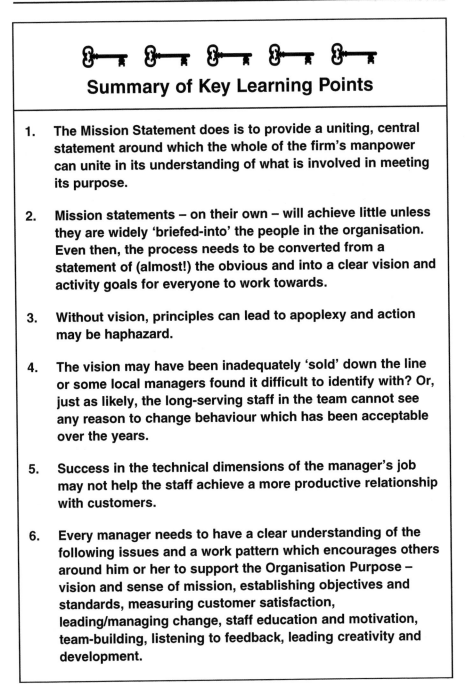

Summary of Key Learning Points

1. The Mission Statement does is to provide a uniting, central statement around which the whole of the firm's manpower can unite in its understanding of what is involved in meeting its purpose.

2. Mission statements – on their own – will achieve little unless they are widely 'briefed-into' the people in the organisation. Even then, the process needs to be converted from a statement of (almost!) the obvious and into a clear vision and activity goals for everyone to work towards.

3. Without vision, principles can lead to apoplexy and action may be haphazard.

4. The vision may have been inadequately 'sold' down the line or some local managers found it difficult to identify with? Or, just as likely, the long-serving staff in the team cannot see any reason to change behaviour which has been acceptable over the years.

5. Success in the technical dimensions of the manager's job may not help the staff achieve a more productive relationship with customers.

6. Every manager needs to have a clear understanding of the following issues and a work pattern which encourages others around him or her to support the Organisation Purpose – vision and sense of mission, establishing objectives and standards, measuring customer satisfaction, leading/managing change, staff education and motivation, team-building, listening to feedback, leading creativity and development.

Summary of Key Learning Points

7. Managers who are not committed themselves will find it difficult to gain the commitment of their team members.

8. 'We are doing it already' or, 'More of the same, really!'. Such statements destroy any vision of improvement – 'crisper service', 'meeting customer's expectations and 'creating customer delight' would be more appropriate!

9. It isn't that a good Retail Manager is just capable of listening – because most of us have all been given two ears – but it may be that we do not use them nearly enough! And we can all use empathy and care to encourage team members to talk to us, but do we hear what is not said as well as what is said?

10. Rewards for a positive Customer Care Development Programme in terms of:
    - team atmosphere and morale
    - individual performance
    - enthusiasm
    - support, automatically provided between team members ...

    ... can be really dramatic – to the extent that managers and team leaders may find themselves wondering how they ever managed before!

Footnote:

The London-based 'Prêt á Manger' fast-food café group publicises its Mission Statement on the front windows of every outlet. It says:

> **Our Mission ...**
>
> **To sell hand-made, extremely fresh food of the highest possible quality. We carefully avoid preservatives, additives and obscure chemicals found in most of the 'prepared' and 'fast' food on the market today.**

PART THREE

MANAGING RETAIL OPERATIONS

'Retail is detail; attention to detail can make all the difference to high quality retail performance.'

Stan Kaufman
(former Managing Director, Allders Department Stores)

10

Products and Services

The case for process and performance standards

1. Introduction

Have you ever had to travel some distance for a special appointment (maybe a business meeting or, perhaps, a training course) and sat increasingly frustrated in a train while some unseen engineer tries to fix a points or signals failure? Your emotions probably followed something akin to the following sequence:

- **Frustration**: 'Why on earth did I decide to travel this way?'
- **Annoyance**: 'Nothing seems to be happening – how long is this going to take?'
- **Anger**: 'Who do they think they are? No one has given us any information – we wouldn't get away with this – why should 'they'?'
- **Retribution**: 'Who can I write/complain to about this?'
- **Fatalism**: 'Everything is the same these days – perhaps we'd be better just staying at home next time.'

Clearly, the unfortunate traveller has suffered through this delay and the provision of information by a sympathetic and well trained Guard or Inspector may reduce the anger and frustration. But nobody can alter the fact that the service, or 'product' has failed.

Customer satisfaction with products and service has been converging over a period of time – and many consumers now find themselves unable to distinguish the serviceability and value of the product itself from the quality of the service which sold it, installed it, repaired it or even disposed of it. For many, the 'product' is the total customer experience over time – not just 'the sale' or a succession of service encounters.

When so much is said in the media about raising quality standards in products, many customers have come to expect that quality in service is also improving; sadly, many are regularly disappointed. This opens the way to considerable competitive advantage to be attained by those businesses who really do 'do-it-better'!

The whole focus of the Quality movement is to ensure that the product or service does not fail – but gives outstanding performance/service and satisfaction.

Case History – 'The best thing we ever bought'

This could be a party game; each person is asked to name a product or service which has given them extreme customer satisfaction. The purpose of the exercise is to contrast amazing value for money against the common items which went wrong (just outside the warranty period, perhaps) and gave the supplier a bad name as a result!

Here is an example:

Our children frequently complained about our kitchen toaster – 'old fashioned' they called its Art Deco shape, and yet it had given amazing service for nearly 20 years. More up-to-date models toasted 4 slices at a time, were made of lightweight plastic rather than metal, and enjoyed 'humidity controls' but our toaster just kept on making toast without failure. Eventually, the day came when the machine expired and had to be replaced. The first replacement – one of the 'new breed' – lasted exactly a fortnight! Its replacement has fared better – but we changed brands, swearing never to buy the failed brand again. Quality and serviceability breeds trust, satisfaction, goodwill and repeat business – and quite a lot of this rubs off on the supplying retailer.

Can you extend this to include consumer experiences of your own or your family and friends?

This chapter seeks to put the customer care process into even sharper focus:

The 'soft' skills are important – but so are the 'promises' made by the products or services you offer!

2. World class v. value for money

What is the purpose of your organisation? We examined this question in Section 2, and by taking a broad view of it. However, we now need to re-examine the positioning of the business – in relation to three factors:

- product quality/value for money
- service level and quality
- price.

Product quality/value for money

At which 'end' of your trade is your business positioned?

For example, in the 'Takeaway/Fast Food' business, we might see the following hierarchy:

- Gourmet Pizza Express (national chain)
- Indian takeaway (local)
- Chinese takeaway (local)
- Harry Ramsden's Fish & Chips
- Kentucky Fried Chicken
- McDonald's
- Burger King
- Fish and Chips (local)
- Sandwich bar (local)

What expectations will customers have of each of these 'brands'? Clearly, each will satisfy the customer's needs (appetites!) but the style and 'promise' of the business will vary according to the image which the business projects. In one case, just the logo of the organisation may be sufficient to project a feeling of trust and value for money. In another, the cheap prices may be accompanied by an expectation of generous portions – even if the food may be eaten from a newspaper package.

Your retail business will have raised expectations from customers, too. A 'no tag' operation will undoubtedly offer value for money, but the absence of a brand label may limit the 'prestige value' of the business and therefore the prices which can be charged. The question is – does the customer know or care?

There is no doubt that image can make a huge difference in the marketability of the product. A simple men's string vest, with the 'right' designer label attached to it may attract a substantially higher selling price than the same article – without a tag – sold in the local market.

Name and place are key elements of the marketing formula!

Would it be any different if the product was shoddy or made of inferior materials, anyway?

The law states that the merchandise must be fit for the purpose intended but the relationship between price and value is 'tested' in the marketplace!

However, blatant exploitation of the public is rarely tolerated for very long, as one major multiple jewellery discovered to their cost after a remarkably candid speech made at what he mistook to be a private function by their Chairman. Clearly, if the business fails to satisfy its customers on this count, they may not remain customers for very long!

The Buying function is confronted with these challenges all the time, and a most important task is to establish reliable sources of supply.

What makes a reliable supplier? Maybe the following factors are seen as important. They provide:

- reliable deliveries
- accurate paperwork
- merchandise which matches the samples shown
- value for money – and
- a cost price which enables a profit to be made.

Just as important – especially when a longer-term relationship is planned – is the continuous improvement of individual lines in the range – and the range itself. As domestic customers increase in sophistication, so they expect retailers (and their suppliers and manufacturers) to adopt new materials, new features and benefits – a process of continuous product improvement.

Retailers obviously risk the tarnishing of their trade reputation with customers if the products they stock and sell prove to be:

- unreliable
- faulty
- poor value for money …

… so, buyers carry considerable responsibility for customer care when selecting new sources of supply.

Service level and quality

Most customers would agree that, whilst Marks and Spencer provide excellent value for money, their main aim is not to provide personal service of the kind which may be found in a private couturier business; their policy is to provide good, efficient 'short service' and this expectation is generally met efficiently.

However, we could also include product availability in this Section. It could be argued that providing polite and quality service has little value if the stock item sought by the customer is actually out of stock.

Would a higher rating be given by the customer if the product was always available (in the appropriate colour, size etc) – even if the quality of service was variable (to say the least)? Such speculation may appear to be of dubious value – obviously customers will be seriously disappointed in your organisation if they are unable to satisfy their needs at your business – and this may have a worse effect when the stock-out is a line which could be considered a basic stock item (for example a 15½" collar white shirt, or a white blouse size 12). Customers can be quite unforgiving if they intended having a barbecue on Bank Holiday Monday – and then discover that everyone in the area has loads of barbecues – but no charcoal!

Finally, service quality may be questioned in a high profile fashion business, in which the 'labels' sold project quality, prestige (and even a little chic glamour), when the staff speak with a common accent with poor grammar – and few manners! (Though this seems to be a selling point in some fashionable restaurants.)

Exclusive retailers operating a virtual monopoly may escape the consequences of customers' negative criticisms in the short term – but it may just be a matter of time … …!

Price

Nobody expects to be able to buy a Rolls Royce at the price of a Mini (if it were possible, the alarm bells might quickly begin to ring.). However, elasticity in pricing depends on a variety of factors:

- customers unaware of the intrinsic value of the product itself
- the lack of local competition on identical or similar merchandise
- the exclusivity and fashion drive behind the design, features and/or brand label attached to the product.

If all the other component parts of the marketing mix are acceptable then the business will flourish. However, the business also needs to protect its position should the market move against the firm – for example through the entry of a new competitor.

3. Reactive marketing

Meeting pressures from competitors with reactive marketing action has been proved necessary for most businesses at some time, although some firms may have decided to adopt a more proactive stance towards change in the marketplace. The question lies in whether it is preferred to lead the market or whether to react and follow other 'players'.

Example 1: Stock availability

In the earlier example, which illustrated the potential damage that stock-outs can cause to the reputation of a business, Senior Managers might well demand better management of stock levels and assortment. Buyers' and suppliers reactions to this may well depend upon the market in which the buyer is working.

In the fashion sectors, the business may be forced to buy stock from suppliers on a 'one-off' basis for the season – with no 'repeats'. Few steps can be taken with systems to support stock control if no repeat orders are possible, anyway. However, buyers do need historical data about stock performance so that they are able to improve their ordering for future seasons.

Pessimism can ultimately cramp the business's performance as much as over-optimism!

Case History

In a completely different field, Argos have one of the most sophisticated information systems for recording demand and matching it with stock data. Computer terminals in the shops record every customer's intended purchase – whether the current stock inventory is able to meet it or not. Compared with most systems this gives significantly more information and can be used to predict future demand (and therefore stock levels needed) in a very sophisticated way.

Smaller businesses – even those with no access to EPOS systems or stock control data – can benefit from simple/manual systems for stock control!

From the perspective of customer service, the lines which are worth controlling closely are those which are:

- in regular demand
- fast sellers
- in the suppliers' stock service catalogue, and/or
- service line categories – which customers expect you to keep in stock.

One related skill which it may be helpful to develop with front-line sales staff is that of 'switch selling' (the ability to sell the customer a viable alternative to the item requested and which is out of stock).

Unless customers are convinced that the alternatives offered will meet their needs or preferences, the overriding impression gained from a stockout may still be one of 'failure'!

In sectors where products are assembled ready for delivery to or collection by, the customer, measures may be easy to apply – but less easy to improve. For example, many 'horror' stories are told of errors and short deliveries in the following situations:

- kitchen units supplied late and incomplete
- wedding list gifts delivered with some listed items missing
- flat-pack furniture supplied with components missing
- quality carpet laid with a poor quality underlay – risking the ultimate effect of the floor covering.

Customers are rarely happy in such situations and may not be readily comforted by the offer of a price reduction.

Even when compensation is agreed, the customer may be left with some experiences which will keep their friends entertained for some time and do absolutely nothing for the good reputation of the business!

Managers can initiate an 'On Time, In Full' (OTIF) measurement with follow-up remedies identified for repeating service failures.

Example 2: The price promise

Businesses that are facing intense local competition have found themselves able to protect their market share by promoting a price promise. This needs to be very carefully thought out and promoted clearly – or more difficulties may be created.

The 'Never Knowingly Undersold' slogan of the John Lewis Partnership is a well-known policy statement in retailing which successfully transmits confidence to customers that their merchandise is not going to appear in cut-price shops locally and, if it does, customers may claim a refund of the difference between their own price and that of the competitor.

Another facet of this kind of scheme lies in the 'no-fuss guarantee scheme' which is operated by some firms (e.g. Argos provides an unqualified 16-day guarantee which covers the eventuality that boxed products may not match the company's standards). Such schemes generate customer confidence.

Case History

Independent department store, Williams & Griffin of Colchester, Essex, adopted a Price Promise policy in 1994 at the bottom of the recession and promoted it widely through point-of-sale, advertising and promotion schemes. The purpose was to promote the business as trustworthy on the price/quality mix, backed with a good standard of service. It was felt that the new policy – also communicated in large window posters, notices to account customers, etc. – would lay to rest any perceptions that Williams & Griffin were expensive and promote the idea that the company looks after their interests best.

Example 3: Setting customer care standards

We have seen that it is quite realistic to use the management tactic of target setting when it comes to price promises and product availability and a similar approach can be adopted when it comes to promoting good service standards. The newly privatised utilities adopted customer service charters in an attempt to underscore the 'new' service standards of customer care being adopted. For example, British Gas established a time target for emergency call-outs with the first 30 minutes without charge and a premium paid to the customer if the engineer failed to attend within 60 minutes. Similar schemes have been applied to other services in more traditional customer service areas. For example, customer service staff in regional builders' merchants, Sharpe & Fisher, were trained to answer telephone enquiries within 3 rings – and to apologise for keeping the customer waiting if the telephone should ring for 3 or more times.

Telephone service standards may seem unnecessarily tough – but they do have impact if every other supplier is doing it and yours is the only firm that is not (and vice versa)!

The following case history gives an example of the kind of 'soft' measures which could be introduced in a selling environment.

Case History

Beatties' Department Stores adopted the following selling standards for sales staff to achieve (this followed an extensive period of training and consultation to achieve full commitment):

Beatties' Customer Service and Selling Standards (extract)

- Acknowledge/approach each customer ideally within one minute of their entering the department,
- Be friendly, enthusiastic and make the customer feel welcome,
- Ask appropriate questions to determine needs,
- Offer merchandise describing its features and benefits,
- Show/suggest related merchandise from your own department or elsewhere in the store,
- Handle the payment process quickly and efficiently, promoting the company account wherever possible,
- Use the customer's name/use your own,
- Offer to transfer merchandise from another store or place a special order if necessary,
- If things go wrong apologise and act quickly to resolve the problem,
- Handle returns graciously and attempt to turn into a sale,
- Keep yourself and your department looking good,
- Make use of the customer database listing system.

Clearly, every trade sector would be able to add some specialist service points to the above extract – for example, to cover mandatory/legal requirements such as Safety/Health warnings or Product Liability.

With the support of departmental managers, this standards approach provides a fundamental syllabus for basic sales and service training and, perhaps more importantly, the basis for performance reviews and counselling!

4. Proactive marketing

New customer service campaigns abound but, as with the long-distance runner, it is the staying power that brings consistent and outstanding results.

Before establishing a new campaign, the business needs to establish 'where it is now' and an important starting point lies in choosing the right measures. Here are some suggestions:

- **Reliability** – the ability to deliver dependably and accurately (see OTIF above)
- **Responsiveness** – willingness to help and provide what is needed
- **Assurance** – ability to generate trust via knowledge and courtesy of staff
- **Empathy** – giving individual attention to customers
- **Tangibles** – giving customer expectations the 'right' physical conditions – e.g. a seat, comfortable changing facilities, appropriate physical layout and environment, etc.

How can the business obtain feedback on which of these factors seem to be failing – or needing improvement? There is a range of Market Research techniques available for the retailer to use (our companion book – *'The Retailer and the Community'* describes Quantitative and Qualitative Research methods in some detail). However, two simple feedback mechanisms which can be very productive, are:

Customer suggestion schemes

To be fully effective, such schemes need to be proactive (not just reactive). In other words, customers need to be encouraged to provide some feedback – perhaps via a competition or money-off vouchers.

Feedback forms and warranty records

Customer feedback, or 'happiness' forms provide a useful means of gathering reactions from customers. However, these reactions may be limited to one aspect of the shopping experience – e.g. the ways in which service excelled (or failed!) and/or the ways that the actual product failed to meet the customer's expectations.

Once again, this kind of method may not achieve much in the way of accurate records of product 'failures'; however, retailers in the furnishings and electrical goods sectors have discovered an innovative way of guaranteeing customer satisfaction – with the retailer earning 'Brownie points', even when the product patently failed or, in some cases, when the product suffered from accidental damage.

Case History

Expanding furnishings retailer, FurnitureLand plc, provides customers with the option of an extended warranty which provides two levels of 'protection': Guardsman protection against 'spills' and 'stains', and 'rips' and 'tears'.

When tested against a product purchase price of anything from a few hundred pounds to several thousand pounds, the customer may obtain 'peace of mind' after the payment of only a fraction of those sums. This can be especially valuable for a customer with a large family, pets etc.

Similar records are kept by a major multiple electrical retailer whose service division provides the service warranties for customers; the primary benefit of this approach is that the retailer has access to unlimited data on product reliability enabling such records to be used in subsequent negotiations with their suppliers.

When retailers enjoy significant buying power, product failures are unlikely to provide a serious financial difficulty for their customers or themselves!

Product guarantees may ensure that retailers provide refunds to their customers but such situations will normally result in a credit from the relevant supplier.

The painful fact is that any product complaint also tarnishes the image of the retailer. This provides a compelling argument for seeking evidence of quality standards employed by all suppliers!

5. Handling customer complaints

Unfortunately, things do go wrong! Whether it be product, system or service failures we have seen that customers are increasingly likely to complain – and probably take the complaint to the very top. Every business needs to take this kind of situation really seriously and ensure that key personnel have been trained in handling disputes by applying the firm's complaints policy. In his bssa book, *'Law for Retailers'* (Management Books 2000 Ltd, 2002), Bill Thomas sets out a recommended procedure for the resolution of disputes and an extract appears below:

Checklist: How to deal with irate customers

- Defuse those feelings
- Smile at customers and say you are sorry
- Take them somewhere private and help them relax
- Ask them to explain what the trouble is
- Ask to see the item so you can form a preliminary view
- Check if the item is one you sell
- Ask when the item was bought and if the customer can remember the sales assistant
- If the defect is obvious and the purchase was in the previous few weeks, ask the customer what he wants.

Summary of complaints procedures

- Train one person to deal with complaints at each location.
- Ensure that staff do not deny they could have sold items.
- All staff should be told (repeatedly) to refer complaints to the complaints person.

(cont)

- The complaints person should have discretion to make refunds up to a limit of, say, £200.
- An unjustified complaint should be rejected politely with a straightforward explanation.
- Ensure staff understand that a complaint is not a reflection on them and not to take them personally.
- Complaints persons must have full information about the relevant Code of Practice and any Conciliation service.
- Managers should try not to overrule decisions by a complaints person.
- Deal with complaints quickly.

Some businesses have established Customer Service Departments (perhaps the name is less provocative than 'Complaints Department'?) who have the responsibility to resolve customers' complaints. Apart from the fact that such a department probably represents a not insubstantial and additional overhead, centralising complaints may not bring an automatic reduction of complaints being generated at the source of the difficulties. There is a lot to be said for ensuring that local managers are given the responsibility of resolving their own complaints – after they have been properly trained, of course.

Case History

British Airways Executive Club (for frequent fliers) was co-ordinated by Carol Mickleborough; Carol's name appeared on some 10 million letters each year so she enjoyed a high profile. One in three complaints were addressed to her personally and the organisation spotted that their customers liked dealing with real people – research showed that one in ten members (60,000 people) believed that they have a personal relationship with Carol! The positive side of all this is that BA noticed a rise in customer satisfaction levels and the company was able to exploit Carol's role by featuring her in group publicity and 'face-to-face' in terminals. The 'secret' in this case is really quite simple – people like to be treated as individuals; they like to know that, when they have something to complain about, there is a real person who will actually do something about it. People are prepared to pay a premium for this kind of service!

6. Summary

Managers need to set high performance standards for products and service policies and train their teams to meet them. Results can then be measured against these standards and corrective action taken when performance falls short. Such development schemes may require substantial time investment initially but, once the scheme is running smoothly, its maintenance will be simpler.

Summary of Key Learning Points

1. When so much is said in the media about raising quality standards in products, many customers have come to expect that quality in service is also improving; sadly, many are regularly disappointed. This opens the way to considerable competitive advantage to be attained by those businesses who really do 'do-it-better'.

2. The 'soft' skills are important – but so are the 'promises' made by the products or services you offer.

3. Name and place are key parts of the marketing formula.

4. The law states that the merchandise must be fit for the purpose intended but the relationship between price and value is 'tested' in the marketplace.

5. Exclusive retailers operating a virtual monopoly and employing poor quality staff, may escape from the results of customers' negative critiques in the short term – but it may just be a matter of time.

6. Pessimism can ultimately cramp the business's performance as much as over optimism.

7. Smaller businesses – even those with no access to EPOS systems or stock control data – can benefit from simple/manual systems for stock control.

8. Unless customers are convinced that the alternatives offered will meet their needs or preferences, the overriding impression gained from a stock-out may still be one of 'failure'.

Summary of Key Learning Points

9. Even when compensation is agreed, the customer may be left with some experiences which will keep their friends entertained for some time and do absolutely nothing for the good reputation of the business.

10. Telephone service standards may seem unnecessarily tough – but they do have impact if every other supplier is doing it and yours is the only firm that is not! (And vice versa.)

11. With the support of departmental managers, a standards approach provides a fundamental syllabus for basic sales and service training and, perhaps more importantly, the basis for performance reviews and counselling.

12. When retailers enjoy significant buying power, product failures are unlikely to provide a serious financial difficulty for their customers or themselves.

13. Product complaints tarnish the image of the retailer. This provides a compelling argument for seeking evidence of quality standards employed by all suppliers.

11

Stock Management

Gold in your hands

1. Introduction

It may seem strange that such a fundamental subject as stock should not appear until Chapter 11 of this book. Throughout, references have been made to its importance – from the selling and customer service viewpoints. This chapter adds the dimension of *profit*.

Most Department and Branch Managers have only limited influence over the range of merchandise which will be stocked (this varies considerably with the size and complexity of the organisation) and it is not the place of this book to address the buying aspects of retailing. However, how much stock is carried – how it should be presented, how much reserve stock there needs to be and how to obtain repeats and/or phased deliveries during the Season, are crucial functions which can affect the sales team's ability to meet sales demand and targets.

Furthermore, good stock-keeping can make a significant difference to the profitability of the operation. Old and damaged stock cannot command expected retail selling prices and mark-downs are usually effective at clearing such stock – but at the expense of the planned margin.

Finally, stock is an attractive commodity – if it wasn't we would not stand much chance of ever selling it! However, this brings its own hazards. Security risks abound and the team has to be vigilant against the possibilities of being the target, both of external thieves and internal fraudsters.

This chapter seeks to provide an overview of the issues involved in stock management – whilst avoiding detailed examination of those systems which are peculiar to each organisation. We will address:

- Stock: an asset or a liability?

- The merchandise sequence
- Control of physical stocks
- Stock accounting
- Stock-turn – the hidden factor
- Visual merchandising and display
- Promotion

As with earlier chapters, there are some suggested activities included from which the reader may learn more about the internal workings of stock management in his or her own organisation.

2. Stock: an asset or a liability?

There are undoubtedly two ways of looking at this – for, since the business exists mainly to supply customer's needs for the kinds of products and services we offer, merchandise is the very life-blood of the organisation. However, depending on the time of the year (the seasons), and whose view we might be taking, we could deduce that either 'label' – asset or liability – is appropriate.

When customer demand is strong and vibrant, we may find ourselves with some doubts as to whether we are likely to have enough stock. In such circumstances, the retailer who has substantial stocks may consider it all to be an 'asset', providing the opportunity to beat sales targets with some ease (and possibly also his local competitors).

The very reverse can also be true. A downturn in customer demand may reveal that we have quite a struggle on hand to achieve our sales targets. In such circumstances, high stocks may be viewed as a liability (at least one major department store group has struggled with this problem through the 90's – carrying progressively older stocks forward from one season to another. This problem was doubly embarrassing as it became public knowledge).

In reality, a varied merchandise range conceals true 'winners' and 'losers' – and it could be argued that the 'winners' are the assets and the 'losers', the liabilities. The successful sales manager is able to exploit the 'winners' by promoting them – at the same time, seeking fair exposure of the less popular lines in the expectation of moving those items within the stock accounting period or season.

Repeat orders can also lead the manager into risky situations – for example, a lawnmower section may have an unbalanced stock in August – with plenty of rotary mowers but few cylinder types. A 'top-up' order could be readily justified. However, with a supply 'lead-time' of two to four weeks, the manager may well find himself with a substantial stock with, perhaps, just six weeks of the main gardening season left.

What happens to the old stock? It may be carried forward into the next year – dormant for, possibly, as many as five or six months. If the department or shop was your business, would you wish to do this?

On the other hand, the customer may be unsatisfied by our existing selection – and, if customer satisfaction is at the heart of our sales policy, what else should we do?

Priority one ...

Extol the virtues of the lines we do have in stock, in the hope that the customer may be prepared to 'switch' to an alternative style, technology, or brand. This assumes that our sales staff have received training on how to do this – but, if successful, we will gain on two counts:

- the stock is reduced by the unit sale and
- no additional stock was added to the stock account.

Priority two ...

The second approach would be to offer to take a special order (if this is realistic from the supply viewpoint). This is less advantageous if there is a minimum order constraint or additional charges made on small orders (thus reducing the profit value of the transaction). However, we would be able to record a 'success' in customer service terms through being able to provide the customer with the preferred product.

The views can therefore shift according to the timing – and also from the perspective of the person who is making the judgement. For example, buyers 'live' in three different seasons:

- last season – with its successes and disappointments
- the present – possibly demonstrating the need to recommend early corrective action (e.g. mark-downs for mid-season Sales)
- the future – range planning and budgeting for the next season.

Their view of the present will undoubtedly be affected by their understanding of what happened in the past and what they understand to be the future trends.

Finance Directors have similar preoccupations but, in their case, it concerns the availability of cash. Cash is needed to fund all the purchasing in the business and is only realised when stock is sold. So, the FD is likely to become increasingly concerned about the liquidity of the business if stocks keep increasing without, at least, a commensurate increase in sales. In such circumstances the non-merchant might be quite entitled to wonder whether the stock isn't a growing liability!

The optimistic sales manager should always try to see the virtues of the current stock range and try to instil these in the sales team. This should build their confidence and bring more sales opportunities!

3. The merchandise sequence

Mistakes can be made in all roles – and this is as true in stock management as in other fields. However, errors in stock management can be exceptionally costly, making the difference between an 'average profit' at the year end – or a very 'handsome return on the year's investment'.

The following diagram illustrates how the sequence normally works and allows us to highlight some of the more obvious risks or errors:

Merchandise System Checklist

ACTION	QUESTIONS
Merchandise inspected	Does it fit into the range? Can we afford it? How much can I sell it for to obtain an adequate return?
Order placed/ Confirmation received	Are all details correct? Are details recorded & committed & money taken off the purchase allowance?
Merchandise arrives	Are goods as ordered? Is there a delivery note? Does it tally with: a) Contents b) Order confirmation?
Merchandise inspected & priced	Is the correct Selling price (SP) applied? Is the margin % recorded?
Invoice arrives	Does the invoice tally with: a) Delivery note b) Confirmation order?
Merchandise put into stock & sold	Is the stock addition noted? Does stock have to be marked down? If so, is mark-down recorded?
Merchandise re-ordered	Is original merchandise decision evaluated?

Obviously, the Unit Manager – on taking up the appointment – assumes responsibility for the stock-in-hand and all that happens to stock in the following periods. Some businesses take stock again at the time when the manager changes (this helps to clarify and ascertain the correct value of the stock on the handover and draws a line beneath any errors occurring under the previous manager). The principles behind this are sound – but it can be disruptive to the business unless the stock count is completed outside normal trading hours.

The above checklist, whilst covering some issues which are the province of the Buyer, helps to identify some of the more obvious points at which stock records can become 'out of sync' with the physical stocks. Such discrepancies can become quite serious at the year end – and therefore need to be controlled carefully throughout the year. For example:

- Has the stock that has just arrived actually been ordered by us? Does it belong to us? Mistakes have been known to be made here – involving stocks which were not nearly as attractive as those selected by the Buyer.
- Are the quantities correct – if not, has an adjustment been recorded (credit note etc),
- Errors in pricing are not so common today with computer records dominating the scene. However, the product may still need ticketing – and mistakes can be made here, too.
- Are supplier's invoices correct against your order (and terms agreed) and the quantities/descriptions of the merchandise delivered? If not there may be an immediate loss or gain on the stock account.
- How careful are we about recording any changes in selling prices – for example discounts allowed on stock items which are slightly 'shop soiled' or on re-pricing older lines as they are overtaken by new stock received at new, higher-selling prices?

Failure to manage these aspects closely can result in very messy situations – and many recriminations – after stock-taking! Some may not actually affect sales – but they will affect profits – and could even help to determine whether your business actually continues to exist in the future!

4. Control of physical stocks

Unit Stock Control

Quite aside from the importance of controlling stocks from the security and protection viewpoints, closer control should bring the possibility of a closer relationship between stocks and customers' demand. This is particularly true of basic stocks which are repeatable (perhaps on a stock and order system) such as hosiery, lingerie or some hardware lines.

There are two approaches to unit stock control:

- Sales Analysis
- Stock Analysis

Sales analysis

The formula for this method is:

OPENING STOCK + DELIVERIES – SALES = CLOSING STOCK

To implement this approach manually:

- stock lines would each be counted at, say, the first month end and the results recorded in a book or on a chart
- delivery units would then be added to the chart as they arrive
- sales for the trading period (say for the next 4 weeks) are then deducted
- the resulting figure should be the closing stock – which can then be audited against actual stocks with a further stock check. Any discrepancies would then be investigated.

This approach is particularly appropriate for stock items which are easily recorded at the service desk or cash point through detachable tickets or scanning devices (used for Electronic Point of Sale [EPOS] systems).

Stock analysis

In this system the process takes a different course:

OPENING STOCK + DELIVERIES – CLOSING STOCK = SALES

- staff count the stock at the end of the 'trading period' (say at the end of the first month)

- again, deliveries are added to the stock record as they arrive
- another stock count (Closing Stock) is carried out at the end of the next month and recorded
- closing stock is then deducted from the total opening stock plus deliveries
- this gives a total, indicating stock which was sold.

This method is particularly appropriate to 'big ticket' sections where the stock is easy to identify and count. For complete accuracy, the final 'Sales' total requires auditing against recorded sales for the period.

Whichever method is adopted, these approaches do bring important side benefits:

Rigorous counting or observation provides a check on stock availability and condition. Such systems, although they are labour-intensive (and possibly less popular with sales staff) demonstrate to everyone that stock is 'gold in their hands' and it must be carefully protected, controlled, maintained and, preferably, sold!

5. Stock accounting

A complementary method of controlling stock is through financial accounting systems. Mostly such systems are senior management tools which are extremely beneficial to the business as a whole, because it is possible to compare actual performance of sales, purchases and expenses control against planned budgets.

Sales accounting is really the simplest part of the equation, as the data can be easily collected – even if profit margins on specific stock lines are not so easily identified.

To obtain a projection of profit performance, it would be possible to multiply sales achieved by the planned profit margin to arrive at a provisional achieved trading profit for the period. Obviously on a company-wide basis this would be very helpful and enable the Management to see how well the firm is doing month-by-month. Such a breakdown might then be made available on a branch or departmental basis enabling specific peaks and troughs of activity to be analysed and possible corrective action undertaken.

On a departmental basis, invoiced merchandise could be presented from the 'Stock Book' and this would typically show:

February Stock Book (all at Selling Price) £000s

Opening Stock value (Brought f/wd from January)	£20,502
Stock additions (Purchases)	£8,500
Total Stock available	£29,002
Less Sales recorded in the Month	£2,100
Closing Stock (Carried f/wd to March)	£26,902

This example illustrates the simplest of stock accounts – set out at selling price and assuming that the 'profit' on sales transactions is actually earned centrally rather than in the department or branch.

A similar approach is adopted in other systems where all the accounts show the value of stock at cost price and the value of sales is 'reduced to cost' through the deduction of the planned margin.

By far the most accurate method of stock management is for records to be maintained simultaneously at both cost and selling price. This enables more thorough control both of the stock value – but also profit margin and the factors which contribute to it (initial price marking, mark-downs, known losses or breakages).With such systems it is quite usual for Sales Managers to be provided with monthly printouts which describe the results from the month's trading (usually against budget). It is obviously essential that the manager thoroughly understands these printouts and can deduce from them any corrective action which may be needed for following periods.

Whichever approach the business uses:

It is essential for sales managers to understand the business's performance accounts thoroughly, and to be able to analyse them arriving at proposed action plans (to exploit or correct strengths and weaknesses)!

6. Stock-turn: the hidden factor

The speed at which stocks are delivered, held in stock and then sold is known as the rate of stock-turn. This is a very important ratio as it provides an insight into the efficiency or productivity of your stock investment. What does it really mean?

Example 1

At its simplest, imagine your shop or department full of stock. Supposing every three months the shop actually sold out all of its stock (i.e. it started Month 1 absolutely full up – sold the stocks well, until running out at the end of Month 3) then the whole process was repeated until the end of Month 12. Obviously, in the full 12 months, we can see that the cycle repeated 4 times (i.e. every 3 months) – so we would expect the Stock-turn figure to be 4.

The precise formula for the rate of stock turn is:

$$\text{RST} = \frac{\text{NET SALES}}{\text{AVERAGE STOCK}}$$

(It is important that both values are at either cost or selling price.)

To arrive at the value for Average Stock, you would normally add together all the month end stock readings and divide by the number of entries.

Example 2

In the example above we had only two records – so we have now added enough to cover a 6-month period:

	Column	February	March	April	May	June	July
Opening Stock	a)	20502	26902	25404	22104	18404	10.104
Plus Stock additions	b)	8500	6100	4250	5200	1100	1575
Total Stock available	c)	29002	33002	29650	27304	19504	11679
Net Sales	d)	2100	7598	7550	8900	9400	7900
Closing Stock	e)	26902	25404	22104	18404	10104	3779

Net Sales for the period were **£43,448**

Average Stock = $\dfrac{\textbf{Addition of Opening Stock for February + Closing Stocks (col. e)}}{\textbf{divided by 7}}$

= £127,199 divided by 7 = £18,171.29

Therefore RST = $\dfrac{\textbf{£43,448}}{\textbf{£18,171}}$ **2.39**

This means that, on average, the business turned its stocks 2.39 times in the year (or was holding approximately 11 weeks stock at any given time) and that the customer is able to choose from nearly three month's stock selection at the height of the trading period.

Of course, in reality, a business will probably never sell quite as much of its stock in quite such a convenient way (although there will probably have been a Summer Sale in the period). Unless you have a pretty rigorous unit stock control system (or a fully computerised stock control system), the calculation of stock-turn will depend upon the collection of 'readings' at significant times of the year. These records can be either expressed as stock units or in financial terms (as shown in the example above).

7. Influencing the stock-turn

As we saw with the earlier example about the lawnmowers, additional stock (even when the item is pre-ordered by customers) can have the effect of increasing our stocks and therefore slowing down our stock-turn. Ideally, to be fully profitable, the business should concentrate its efforts on those stocks which move fastest – at a good profit margin – and remove the slow sellers from the range entirely.

In practice this may not be quite so possible – as some of the slow-sellers will be 'service lines' which help attract customers to buy the main items from your business. The challenge is illustrated in the following chart on page 183.

Good stock control systems should ensure that there are simple re-order systems to ensure that stock-outs are avoided on both the Fast Seller and Basic Demand Lines categories. Positive customer dissatisfaction is likely to result if the customer catches you out of stock in either category!

This is where the computer pays for itself over and over again. With the benefit of historical demand data, a simple unit stock control system will also recommend the ideal number of units to be kept in stock to meet predicted demand. This will help avoid the build up of 'squirrel stocks' – kept 'just in case' a customer may ask for them (adopting this policy across a large range can cripple the stock-turn figure and leave the business overstocked with increasingly old and shop-soiled items).

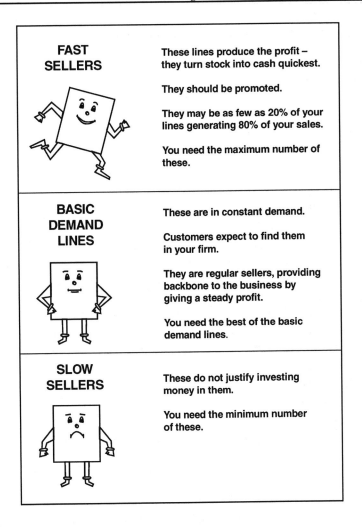

 **FAST SELLERS** 	These lines produce the profit – they turn stock into cash quickest. They should be promoted. They may be as few as 20% of your lines generating 80% of your sales. You need the maximum number of these.
BASIC DEMAND LINES	These are in constant demand. Customers expect to find them in your firm. 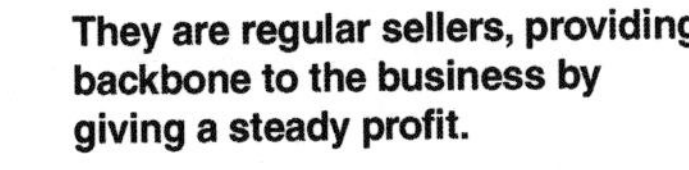They are regular sellers, providing backbone to the business by giving a steady profit. You need the best of the basic demand lines.
SLOW SELLERS 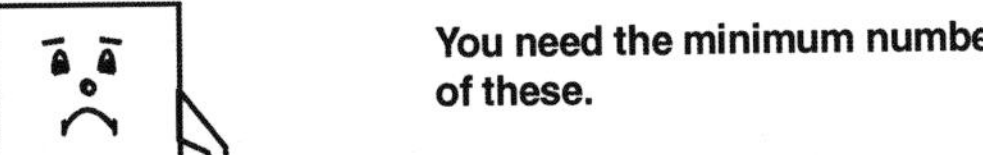	These do not justify investing money in them. You need the minimum number of these.

The 'modern' approach to stock control is to ensure that it is in stock 'just-in-time' when it is needed by customers. This approach may be difficult to implement in some departments but integrating stock and order systems with suppliers' own systems can achieve improvements in customer service and faster stock-turn!

8. Visual merchandising and display

As we have seen, generating an improvement in sales can be achieved by a number of factors as well as through any general up-surge of customer demand that every retailer seeks.

The presentation of the shop and the stock, in particular, can have a dramatic effect on the way in which the business is seen by the customer. Space only allows a brief look at these two factors but any Sales Manager can learn a great deal about eye-catching techniques simply by walking around a successful shopping centre.

Here are some tips about your window displays.

Display

Consider how long it takes for a customer to pass your windows. In some cases it may simply be a matter of a few seconds. In that time, the windows are expected to catch the customers' attention and simply demand that they pause to take in what is shown in the window – then, hopefully, take the decision to come into the shop. After that, it is all down to the Merchandising layout and the skills of the sales team.

In the first instance, we need to keep our feet on the ground – it might be nice to present our business as if it is in Knightsbridge or Bond Street but our target (or existing) customers could be put off by that image (just as they might be by a 'market trader' image).

Here are some fundamental check points:

Checklist 1: Fundamentals

- Every window should seek to 'sell' to the customer,
- You do not have to be an artist to be able to prepare good windows (it is not an esoteric skill.)
- Display space is being paid for anyway, so it should be made to earn its keep.
- Windows are really unpaid sales people.
- The display is the medium, not the message – do not try to be too clever!

It is very important that the display is properly planned if time and energy is to pay off; the best way of doing this is to make some notes on what you wish to achieve – well before the set time when you are to carry out the project. (Otherwise there is a risk that you may find some of the ingredients on your 'recipe' are missing when you come to use the mixture.)

Here is a Planning Checklist:

Checklist 2: Planning

Choose a theme and make a plan – keep it simple. Consider:

- To whom is the display to be addressed?
- What do you wish to show? (Don't try to put everything in the window – it will simply confuse the customer)
- What physical difficulties will you need to overcome? (e.g. height, support, suspending merchandise, units etc)
- What display equipment and props are needed/available?
- How can we ensure good lighting for the display? (Will we need the help of an electrical technician?)
- Will the display benefit from graphics, posters, captions etc? (How will we obtain them?)

This checklist should help make a start on your plans. The next task is to plan out the composition of the window. Here is another checklist:

Checklist 3: Display composition

Theme:

- Decide your theme, for example, will it be Seasonal? Will it present the merchandise in an appropriate way, e.g. a Christmas presentation will attract the eye if it also includes some discreet gift boxes, decorations etc.

Balance

- Will you use Symmetrical or Asymmetrical balance? Do you wish to group the merchandise or present it in random order? (cont)

Colour

- Most flexibility will be in the back-drops and/or pedestal colouring. For example, that Christmas window will be most effective if it uses reds, gold, silver etc. “Female” colours such as pinks, blue and light green will be appropriate contrasting with the browns, greys and navies often associated as “male” colours.

Lighting

- Additional spotlighting makes a dramatic difference in highlighting a display. Spotlights can also be used to pick out specific merchandise – best done from above. Specialist electrical help may be needed to wire up any additional lighting.
- Please do not forget that good displays are often spoiled if they are poorly maintained.

A good display should be changed fortnightly; apart from anything else, the merchandise will become soiled or faded if it is left any longer than this!

Finally, it is amazing how much you can learn from other people’s displays. Decide for yourself what seems to work and which displays have most impact.

Merchandising

Merchandising is the technique of presenting products for sale in such a way that it attracts people and persuades them to buy. It concerns the ‘Five Ps’:

*** Products * Presentation * Persuasion * People * Purchasing**

Products

Some products sell themselves; for example, colour is a very strong motivator and the way in which a colour assortment is presented can attract customers (e.g. the paintbox approach – or using the colour mix as it is seen in the rainbow). Related products, if shown alongside the primary products, can motivate impulse purchases – for example the tie with the shirt, the handbag with the shoes.

If there are special style features on/with the product, they need to be made readily obvious, or the customer's attention may not be caught.

The product mix and sizing must be right for customers to be motivated to make initial selections. Benefiting from impulse purchasing means that the product must be available now.

Careful thought should be given to the 'entry offer' in the shop or department. This needs to be visually strong enough to attract customers to explore further into the shop.

Presentation

Visual merchandising racks should be neatly presented – but not to the point that customers have the feeling that they are not supposed to disturb anything! (Supermarkets use 'starter gaps' to overcome this difficulty). The overall atmosphere of the business should be considered, too. Is it inviting, warm/cool, with some signs of activity and not too noisy?

How can you gain impact through the use of bulk displays? Can your fixturing be used to encourage customers to get in amongst the stock – or is this a disincentive?

Finally, the products need to look fresh – packaging must be clean, tidy, unbroken boxes, with clear labelling and correct merchandise in correct places.

Persuasion

There are, undoubtedly, 'hot spots' in every shop layout – places which seem to attract nearly every browsing customer. The question is, is it the merchandise which always attracts visitors to this position? Or is it something to do with the fixturing?

Either way, these positions are the places which you should be consciously using to promote your fast sellers (those items, perhaps which carry higher profit margins). Positions at eye level in the department are also high impact areas – it is interesting to note that customers' attention nearly always starts at this level. Once again, the stock presentation should benefit from this.

Colours and merchandise should always be co-ordinated in the presentation so that the customer has least amount of effort in relating individual product lines within the overall 'family' of the range. (Customers always buy when you make it easier for them).

Stock should be presented in the ways in which it might be used in real life – so, for example, the front jacket on a rack should be presented 'front-facing' with all the related accessories – the shirt and tie – or blouse and scarf, and perhaps some simple jewellery!

This approach parallels those mouth-watering 'serving suggestions' you can find on the outside cartons of those 'TV Meals' you will find in the freezer section of your favourite supermarket!

People

People can be very resistant to the idea of being 'talked into something they did not want'; but are often very happy to browse and even try some of your merchandise for size, comfort, or style. This means that the sales team need to be adept at getting into casual conversation with customers with snippets of product and style information and general conversation about subjects of common interest. (This skill is described in our companion book – 'Retail Selling').

We all have a strong desire to touch merchandise and it is often possible to get a good picture of the items which attract customers – just by observing their reactions to feel the merchandise and weigh up the comfort factors.

Customers love to feel that they are individuals – and this is a good reason for not putting all the look-alike sized products out on display. The last thing people want to feel is that everyone else in the community is probably going to be wearing this product!

Purchases

Sales will undoubtedly go up if your sales team is able to identify when browsing customers suddenly become potential customers who need some service and a little encouragement. The team needs to be know how to convert a casual enquirer into an enthusiastic purchaser.

For maximum impact, the products customers wish to buy need to be available for purchase, now. (The longer the delay, the more chance the customer has to 'go cold' on the purchase) and, please, do ensure that as few obstacles are placed in their way as possible when they actually come to pay!

Remember that the image you tried to project through your window displays (prestigious, exclusive etc) will carry so much more impact if all the other parts of the service match this. This might include, for example, some gift wrapping or special packaging as part of the service!

Finally, all this can make a big effect on your reputation and sales performance. Some research carried out to measure the effectiveness of in-store merchandising, in comparison with other marketing methods, when it comes to persuading customers to buy, showed:

In-store merchandising	44%
Newspaper advertisements	26%
TV commercials	20%
Magazine advertisements	10%

So, your efforts on visual merchandising are important!

9. Promotions

It is often thought that the most effective way of increasing sales activity is to run a promotion for a short while – an event!

Your plan could include the offer of a special mid-season promotional discount and, on the face of it, the event could be really effective. The problem with this is that, come next year if the same thing happens with trade, the temptation is to repeat the same kind of event and, before too long, we have created an out-of-season discount plan and unwittingly contributed to the possible down-grading of the image of the business.

This is not to say that promotions are wrong. Perhaps, for an up-market fashion business, the 'discount budget' could be applied in a different way in the form of, say, an 'Italian Wine and Cheese' evening for account customers. This kind of approach will work when the business already has a close rapport with its customers (and perhaps a database listing).

The precise timing of the seasonal Sale is another decision which can create real dilemmas in the business. While the larger businesses in the area compete for early Sales dates, there may be something to be said for a very late Sale – a true 'End of Season' clearance. Here are some arguments for an individual policy for the individual business.

A distinctive feature of well managed promotions is the degree of preparation put into promotion events – including, of course, the proper briefing of the sales team!

Unfortunately this aspect is the one which is so often overlooked.

10. Summary

This chapter has sought to remind the manager of some of the critical physical approaches to good stock management. It could be said that some of the issues covered have assumed to be instinctive in good retail managers. This may sometimes be true. However,

Retailing is also very much a 'scientific' industry – depending upon astute financial control and investment strategy. These functions can be completely destroyed if local managers do not have the necessary skills and understanding to attract customers and satisfy their needs!

Summary of Key Learning Points

1. The optimistic sales manager should always try to see the virtues of the current stock range and try to instil these in the sales team. This should build their confidence and bring more sales opportunities.

2. Failure to manage stock and stock records closely can result in very 'messy situations' – and many recriminations – after stock-taking. Some problems may not actually affect sales – but they will affect profits – and could even help to determine whether your business actually continues to exist in the future.

3. Rigorous counting or observation provides a check on stock availability and condition. Such systems, although they are labour-intensive (and possibly less popular with sales staff), demonstrate to everyone that stock is valuable and it must be carefully protected, controlled, maintained and, preferably, sold.

4. It is essential for sales managers to understand the business's performance accounts thoroughly, and to be able to analyse them arriving at proposed action plans (to exploit or correct strengths and weaknesses).

5. Good stock control systems should ensure that there are simple re-order systems to ensure that stock-outs are avoided on both the Fast Seller and Basic Demand lines categories. Positive customer dissatisfaction is likely to result if the customer catches you out of stock in either category.

Summary of Key Learning Points

6. The 'modern' approach to stock control is to ensure that it is in stock 'just-in-time' when it is needed by customers. This approach may be difficult to implement in some departments but integrating stock and order systems with suppliers' own systems can achieve improvements in customer service and faster stockturn.

7. A good display should be changed fortnightly; apart from anything else, the merchandise will become soiled or faded if it is left any longer than this.

8. Some products sell themselves; for example, colour is a very strong motivator and the way in which a colour assortment is presented can attract customers (e.g. the paintbox approach – or using the colour mix as it is seen in the rainbow). Related products, if shown alongside the primary products, can motivate impulse purchases – for example the tie with the shirt, the handbag with the shoes etc.

9. Stock should be presented in ways in which it might be used in real life – so, for example, the front jacket on a rack should be presented 'front-facing' with all the related accessories – the shirt and tie – or blouse and scarf, and perhaps some simple jewellery.

10. Customers love to feel that they are individuals – and this is a good reason for not putting all the look-alike sized products out on display. The last thing people want to feel is that everyone else in the community is probably going to be wearing this product.

Summary of Key Learning Points

11. Remember that the image you tried to project through your window displays (prestigious, exclusive etc) will carry so much more impact if all the other parts of the service match this. This might include, for example, some gift wrapping or special packaging as part of the service.

12. A distinctive feature of well managed promotions is the degree of preparation put into promotion events – including, of course, the proper briefing of the sales team.

13. Retailing is also very much a 'scientific' industry – depending upon astute financial control and investment strategy. These functions can be completely destroyed if local managers do not have the necessary skills and understanding to attract customers and satisfy their needs!

12

Managing the Budget

More on the money business

1. Introduction

Ultimately, running a business successfully comes down to the question of money – how to make the best of the resources and achieve the best results. If this seems a little stark, the truth is that Retailing has always had the reputation of being a money-oriented industry – make plenty of money for the Company and you will be well regarded. This at least provides a common measurement point for everyone – removing some of the favouritism which can characterise organisations which are not so financially oriented.

This chapter is aimed at helping the Sales Manager gain a better understanding of the factors which contribute to good 'bottom line results'. Factors covered are:

- the branch or department diary
- branch/department accounts
- wages, commission and overheads
- productivity and staff scheduling
- capital expenditure
- communications.

2. The branch or department diary

Most experienced Sales Managers have learned the value of keeping a 'Trading Diary' in which useful trading information is recorded. It is amazing how short our memory is – even from month to month (let alone what happened at this time last year – or even the year before!) – and it is valuable to record just enough detail to explain what was happening at the time. A good vehicle for this valuable record would be a 'page-a-day' diary – or, if available, a 'perpetual desk diary' (one which has dates but no days marked). In this way, up to 5 years trading data (e.g. takings and any team changes) could be recorded and some simple, related data such as changes in bank interest rates, the weather and promotions.

This may seem like a chore but there is no doubt that it will pay for itself once the first year is completed.

The future can only be forecast from the past, so details of past trading will prove very valuable as time goes on!

3. Branch or department accounts

As we have seen in the previous chapter, most well managed retail businesses produce a set of management accounts at least monthly – and these will almost certainly include a breakdown of performance on a department-by-department basis. Under normal circumstances these departmental or branch accounts would be distributed to the Sales Managers concerned so that the team's performance can be monitored – and corrective action proposed. (If the reader does not see such statements or printouts then perhaps you should ask your manager if you can see them – and ask if you can be coached in what they show at the same time. The logic for this is that, if managers are to be able to contribute towards achieving an improvement in performance, they need to know what they are up against and what kind of performance is needed to make the business grow).

Specifically, while it is probably not possible for the manager to have any effect on the fixed overheads of the unit, it is helpful to understand the level of sales activity which is needed for the section to achieve in order that 'break-even' point can be met and profits then earned. This break-even point is the point at which profits earned overtake the fixed costs of the operation).

The following report illustrates the type of accounts which might be available to the manager.

		1-Feb	2-Mar	3-Apr	4-May	5-Jun	6-Jul	Season
Opening Stock	Budget	233,000						233,000
	Actual	210,657						210,657
	Variance	-22,343						-22,343
Sales	Budget	47,900	73,800	86,000	56,500	62,600	75,000	401,800
	Actual	51,376	73,009	65,481	44,139	58,535	61,182	353,722
	Variance	3,476	-791	-20,519	-12,361	-4,065	-13,818	-48,078
Markdowns	Budget	-1,500	-900	-1,000	-100	0	2,000	-1,500
	Actual	-1,724	-662	-149	156	4,922	-761	1,782
	Variance	-224	238	851	256	4,922	-2,761	3,282
Shrinkage	Budget	0	0	0	0	0	0	0
	Actual							
	Variance							
Purchases	Budget	44,000	74,000	86,000	57,000	63,000	63,000	387,000
	Actual	36,623	91,623	90,999	55,568	40,093	60,989	375,895
	Variance	-7,377	17,623	4,999	-1,432	-22,907	-2,011	-11,105
Closing Stock	Budget	230,600	231,700	232,700	233,300	233,700	219,700	219,700
	Actual	197,628	216,904	242,571	253,844	230,480	231,048	231,048
	Variance	-32,972	-14,796	9,871	20,544	-3,220	11,348	11,348
Sales last year		43,549	67,066	78,219	51,338	56,894	68,143	365,209
Sales growth%	Budget 10.0%	Actual 18.0%	Actual 8.9%	Actual -16.3%	Actual -14.0%	Actual 2.9%	Actual -10.2%	Actual -3.1%

The sample shown provides a very clear statement of departmental sales performance over a six month period. It also enables the manager to pinpoint outstanding performance and any potential problems which may need action. For example, this report shows that problems began to hit the section in Period 3, from which sales never recovered. Clearly some action needed to be taken at that time and failure to do so led to:

- sales £48,000 down on target
- closing stock £11,000 over target.

Clearly the situation could have been worse had purchasing not been controlled carefully in periods 4-6.

For higher levels of control, the manager would also need to receive a report on profit margin and stock-turn. These items then would give a complete picture of the 'health indicators' for the business.

If you receive printouts like this, you probably already know what to do with them but, in case this is not so, here are some suggested courses of action:

- Check the figures against your own records to ensure that the printout has correctly credited the sales (errors have been known to occur and the printout will almost certainly be taken as correct unless you query it with your manager)
- Compare this month's performance on sales and gross profit with your target or forecast and note any differences (together with any explanations for outstanding or poor performance)
- Either way, it is then wise to refer back to the previous year to check what performance was like for the same period – again noting any particular reasons why this year should have been better or not as good (for example there may have been more trading days in the period this or last year, or the weather may have been exceptionally bad last year – and this year you are benefiting from a heatwave.).
- The next step is to look to see what the printout can tell you about the budget for the year. If the section is 'up' then can this trend be held, and if so, what action needs to be taken (more stock? better displays? another advertisement?). Similarly, can you be ready to propose a suitable action plan if trade results are disappointing?
- Finally (and perhaps most importantly), the direct expenses of the unit should be examined and the effect of these, and any other expenses charged to the unit, re-examined. The question should be asked 'Are we getting good value from these costs – are they being satisfactorily delivered at present – could the services be obtained in any more cost-effective way?'

This trading analysis should be carried out soon after the printout is received (not put on the pile or in that 'useful' folder for consideration 'sometime when I have the time') and, when it is completed, it would be a good idea to telephone your manager for an opportunity to discuss how you feel about it (rather than waiting for the manager to contact you). That conversation should be helpful in letting you know how your team's performance compared with others in the Company, what others have made of current trading conditions, and if there are any other ideas/plans you have not considered which will help you maintain or improve current trading performance.

When this whole process is complete you should call a briefing meeting of your team to thank them – and encourage them to even greater efforts for the next period.

Effective Sales Managers are proactive, not reactive; they study performance and ask why things are as they are? And how to improve them? They consult everyone involved – giving credit where it is due! Don't wait to be asked for a report – offer your analysis first!

3. Wages, commission and overheads

After the occupancy costs (usually, mostly rent) involved in the business are met, and the merchandise is paid for, the next most substantial cost is that of staffing the unit.

When expressed in financial terms, this may not seem a large element but, when it is expressed as a percentage of sales (in common with all the other expense elements), the salary bill may vary from as low as 8%

(typically in a self-service operation, which runs 'light' on sales staff) rising to as high as 15-16% (in a strong personal service operation). Industry 'norms' are of little benefit here, since the business needs to relate the costs to the returns gained from the sales team – and the customer service strategy which the business is following. However, there is also the need to keep a close eye on trends in the local labour market (or else some very capable staff may start leaving for better rates offered by local competitors!).

Payment-by-results has been briefly discussed in Chapter 6 and, from a budgetary point of view, its value as part of the company's motivation system can, perhaps, now be better appreciated. If we pay more to staff in their basic wages – will this bring an increase in sales performance? If we were to provide a simple commission system and relate this to some specific targets, might they make more consistent efforts to achieve the targets?

Such targets could include:

- achieving additional sales above the planned target
- increasing the number of related sales made to existing customers
- encouraging customers to take out an extended guarantee or warranty
- selling accessories to go with the primary purchase (e.g. polish and trees to go with the shoes).

There is little doubt that this approach does work – and many staff enjoy the sense of friendly competition that can be created. (The manager needs to keep an eye on this to see that it does not get out of hand and start to affect customer relations, though. And a fair and accurate system must be set up to ensure that the right people gain the rewards to which they are entitled.).

Case Histories

- The Richer Sounds organisation uses a significant range of incentives to staff to encourage strong involvement in the business – from cash payments under a Suggestion Scheme to the loan of the Chairman's white Rolls-Royce for the weekend in cases of outstanding performance.
- A major growth area of the Marks and Spencer group are the Reward Vouchers which employers are able to use as incentives to their staff.

(cont)

Case Histories (cont)

- On a more global scale, the Air Miles and Loyalty Points systems (e.g. Nectar) tacked onto petrol sales and selected shopping have undoubtedly affected people's views of incentives of one kind or another. The employee incentive market is now said to be worth £700M a year – a major business in its own right.
- Bruno Frey, Professor of Economics at the University of Zurich, argues that, for an incentive to work, it needs to be related to the needs of the whole group of employees and be designed to enhance team motivation and morale as well as providing a reward to the individual. Otherwise, incentives can just become an ineffectual contribution to the general overheads of the organisation.

4. Productivity and staff scheduling

Now that we have begun to review the performance of our sales staff, we might delve a little further into areas of productivity.

The improvement of staff productivity in the business has only a relatively recent history in retailing – starting with some early Work and Method Studies carried out in the Hardware department of a department store in the 1950s. Since then, the arrival of Selective Employment Tax in the 1960s and, more recently, the adoption of 7-day trading (and shift working) has created a move of emphasis away from how staff time should be used to when are they needed to be here? The outcome of this has been to consider the greater use of part-timers in the business – and relate their hours more closely to when they are needed to provide 'live customer service work' (in other words, when customers are actually present and need their service). As with many other challenges of this kind – there are both advantages and disadvantages to the approach.

The principal advantage is that the heavy overhead of staff costs is reduced so that, in general, staff are only brought into the shop when they are actually needed and they can earn their 'keep'.

The main disadvantage, if this idea were taken to the extreme, is that the various non-selling duties which are needed to be carried out may not be carried out satisfactorily if there are not sufficient people in attendance. (Obviously, the counter argument to this is that the rostering should be flexible enough to cover for this need.)

Example

How might this work?

A payroll budget would be produced first (this budget might be set at, say, 9.5% of sales value). In a given month, with a Sales Target of £20,800 this would give an actual figure of £1,976 for the Branch. Deducting the manager's salary of £1,500, just £476 would be available in the staff budget. Dividing this by a standard hourly rate (say, £4 per hour) the budget will 'buy' 119 hours work. With an opening schedule of 52 hours, this would produce an equivalent number of full-time staff of 2.3.

So, the Branch would be operated by a manager and 2 full-time sales persons (+ a part-timer).

However, this might not be the best way of spending the payroll budget.

A study of the pattern of trade may show the key times when the shop is busiest and when the greatest staff support may be needed. As an example, the following plan could provide a good balance for the staff schedule:

	Manager	**Sales FT**	**Sales PT**	**Sales PT**	**Sales PT**
Monday 9-5.30	H	X	-	X	-
Tuesday 9-5.30	X	X	X 11-4pm	-	-
Wednesday 9-5.30	X	H	X 11-4pm	-	-
Thursday 9-7pm	X	X	X 11-4pm	X 3-7pm	X 5-7pm
Friday 9-6pm	X	X	X 11-4pm	-	-
Saturday 9-6pm	X	X	X 11-4pm	X	X
		45 hrs	25 hrs	20 hrs	12 hrs

Total Hours = 102 hrs

Allowing an additional 17 hrs in reserve for staff sickness, holiday cover etc.

(X = attending the business)

Assignment

If you have not produced a similar Schedule to this, it would be a useful task to carry out. For best results you will need some data on the current pattern of trade i.e. % sales achieved on each day of the week and the percentage split across the hours of each day. The real salary costs need to be used (including any employee overheads involved) for the calculation to be accurate. When you have a new staffing schedule, ask your Manager to discuss it with you – and also the challenges involved in changing the hours of existing staff.

Staff scheduling can provide a useful way of raising staff productivity – the theory being that sales people should be present when they are most likely to be selling to customers!

In reality, the figure work is not the only dimension to this task – the correct identity of 'key hours' to be covered in the business is very important (in the above example it was felt to be 11-4pm). (Additional resources may also be needed to cover for days when deliveries will be received – or other non-selling duties need to be undertaken).

The geography of the sales floor also has an important effect on the staffing – for example – does the shop trade on 1, 2 or even 3 floors? How easily can the sales floor be covered (especially from the Security viewpoint) – are there any hidden corners/cashpoints that have to be staffed all the time? or changing rooms that need to be supervised?

5. Capital investment

All managers like to feel that their shop benefits from the most up-to-date fixturing and decor; the problem is that re-fits can be exceptionally expensive (possibly as much as £65 per square foot) and, in some sectors, the effects may only last as little as five years.

At a recent Merchandising workshop, the managers of some furnishing superstores were competing with each other over the age of their carpets!

This was a harmless 'game' until one of their number announced that he had a new one in his store – everyone wanted to know how he had managed to persuade his Senior Manager to provide it.

The sheer cost of such investments make it understandable that Senior Managers have to think more than twice before going into a major refurbishment. However, failure to invest can leave the business looking dowdy and will eventually have an effect on its image and sales performance.

Re-fitting in a large business is something like painting the Forth Bridge. The constant re-cycling of floor plans, re-investment in new fixturing, provision of walk-ways, not to mention ensuring the right ambience with the lighting provision is a major role and one which has to be taken really seriously.

However, the decision to invest has to be made in parallel with the consideration of the likely payback which the project will bring about!

If this is in doubt then the business may be fighting against an increasingly strong tide (e.g. when the 'shopping centre' moves from one focal point to another, and the Management are faced with a rearguard action). Sound management techniques do not have much to offer in such circumstances – a long-term strategy was really needed when the shopping developments were first mooted.

Financing for these kinds of capital projects is a specialised business. However, some broad principles can be recorded.

- New fixtures and fittings are usually depreciated at a rate of 10% per year.
- An assessment needs to be made of how much additional profit will be earned as a result of the investment (without any 'kidology'!).
- Consideration must also be given to how quickly this extra profit is likely to be earned.

The ultimate goal is to assess the payback period – i.e. the time it will take to recoup the initial investment (remembering that the longer it takes the less value the money will have in today's terms.)

6. Communications

As we have seen, there are a wide number of factors that can affect the survival and expansion of the business over a period of time. Some are things which we have considerable influence over – the factors which we can change and develop inside the business.

However, from time to time the manager (and the business) will be hit by external 'squalls' – some of which should have been predicted, and others may have been quite unpredictable.

Good communications are essential in this 'game' of keeping one step ahead of rapidly-changing market conditions. Local managers have a special duty to keep up-to-date with any local plans for new schemes (e.g. pedestrianisation, the proposed removal of bus-stops and zebra crossings, changes such as the abolition of free parking in town centres). It is much easier for local staff to keep informed about such proposals than executives who may be in some remote corner of the enterprise, located elsewhere in the country. It is very important that 'local intelligence' is passed upwards to enable the right levels of representation to be made.

As has already been stated in Part 2, the sales team should be properly briefed about all matters which are likely to contribute to the 'health and fitness' of the business – including investment plans and any threat to the continued existence of the business.

Your team may not be shareholders but they are stakeholders, and therefore can make a substantial difference to its long-term success; they should be taken into your confidence, and briefed accordingly!

7. Summary

This chapter has contributed an overview of a vitally important aspect of the manager's job. Hopefully, it will also serve as an 'appetizer' for a further, in–depth study of the subject for which the reading list will help (see Appendix).

Summary of Key Learning Points

1. The future can only be forecast from the past, so details of past trading will prove very valuable as time goes on.

2. Effective Sales Managers are proactive, not reactive; they study performance and ask why things are as they are? And how to improve them? They consult everyone involved – giving credit where it is due. Don't wait to be asked for a report – offer your analysis first!

3. Staff scheduling can provide a useful way of raising staff productivity – the theory being that sales people are present when they are most likely to be selling to customers.

4. The geography of the sales floor also has an important effect on the staffing – for example – does the shop trade on 1, 2 or even 3 floors? How easily can the sales floor be covered (especially from the Security viewpoint) – are there any hidden corners/cashpoints that have to be staffed all the time? or changing rooms that need to be supervised?

5. The decision to invest has to be made in parallel with the consideration of the likely payback which a project will bring about.

6. Your team may not be shareholders but they are stakeholders, and therefore can make a substantial difference to its long-term success; they should be taken into your confidence, and briefed accordingly.

13

Safety First!

Looking after your staff, customers and the environment

1. Introduction

It is a dangerous world we live in – but perhaps, in various ways, it always has been. Whilst we have become much more accustomed to behaving responsibly when it comes to protecting our fellow human beings – there are still some pretty awful accidents causing injuries, and worse, which often narrow down to someone's negligence (or everyone leaving the control of hazards to someone else).

On average, ten people are killed in accidents at work every week and about two million have illnesses which may be work related. Quite aside from the guilt involved after an accident which could, perhaps, have been avoided, the community – your community – never quite recovers from the occurrence. A public event lives on in people's memory for a long, long time. (The infamous fire in the furnishing section in a Manchester store is a first class example of this – as it is always quoted as a particularly bad case, with some fatalities from the poisonous smoke and considerable difficulties experienced in evacuating the building).

What has been different in the last 20 years or so is the protection which should be extended to staff of, and visitors to, the premises of the business. All this has come about as a result of the Health and Safety at Work Act, and the subsequent implementation of various regulations under the Act. Things have got a lot better – but we are all human and mistakes are made – sometimes with very costly results. So, this chapter is intended to act as a reminder for all Sales Managers and here is a first learning point:

Never overlook the regulations on Health and Safety, they are intended for everyone's protection!

2. The needs

The 1974 Health and Safety at Work etc Act placed a variety of general duties both on employers and their employees not to act in any way which might threaten the health and safety of all staff and visitors to the site – and particularly in relation to the provision of information, instruction and training.

This means that, in your department or branch, it is the manager's responsibility – as a representative of the employer, to ensure that staff are properly instructed about risks or hazards which the manager knows may exist or could occur in the future. In practice, most firms have a standard Induction Training programme or checklist (see Chapter 4) and this will emphasise those points which are most likely to apply in your business. However, it is also necessary (and sensible) to ensure that hazards and precautions are re-emphasised from time to time – and also if/when any systems of work are changed, or new risks are introduced to which employees may be exposed. Here is a vital topic for inclusion in a formal team-training session.

In retailing and distribution, one of the key risks for which team members may need training reminders is materials handling – especially if your staff are expected to help unload lorry deliveries (for example before the Sale) – or maybe putting stock away, perhaps on the top of fixtures (involving the use of ladders or steps).

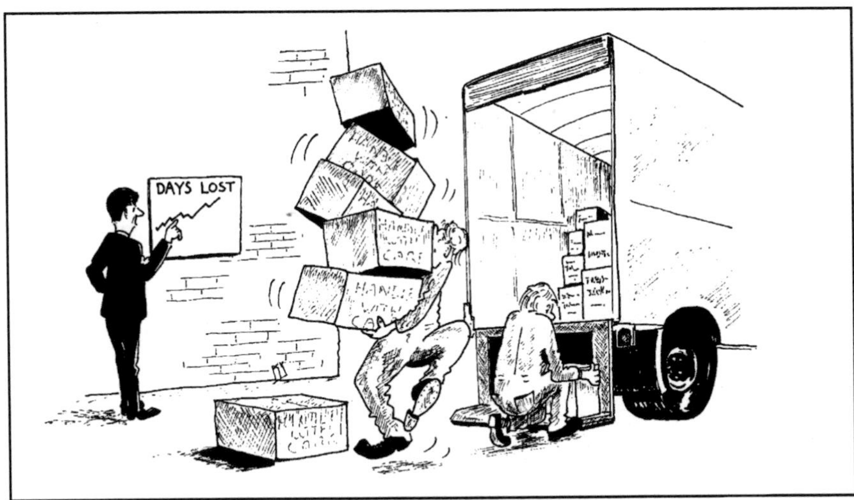

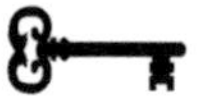

Millions of pounds sterling are lost every year in the UK as a result of back injuries as people fail to follow simple lifting rules – all very easy to do when enthusiasm overtakes good lifting technique!

3. Sickness absence

From time to time, figures are published on the cost of absenteeism to British industry. A recent CBI survey identified the cost as £10.5 billion and recommended employers consider what action they could take to reduce this. The survey estimated that 187 million working days were lost due to sickness in 1999 (3.4% % working time) and suggested:

'The key to successful absence control is giving responsibility to the first line manager to monitor absenteeism. Employees are too often considered to be an expendable resource. The increase in absenteeism reported among non-manual staff often arises from low morale and motivation, largely caused by uncertainty over job security and lack of investment in staff development'.

The Health Education Authority's Health at Work Award is awarded to firms which promote a national health quality standard; this is particularly important in these days of stress, which contributes to so much illness and sickness absence.

Managers need to exercise leadership by counselling team members when they have been absent from work – especially discussing the additional pressures that absence places on other team members!

4. Hazard spotting

Managers need support with their responsibility for ensuring a hazard-free working environment and this is a good reason for recruiting team members as hazard spotters. The kinds of items which might arise – which should be reported for further action – could typically include:

- boxes blocking aisles/doorways/fire exits
- stretched cables – placing strain on power sockets/leads for electrical equipment

- hygiene risks associated with poor maintenance/usage of toilets and washing facilities
- premises which are either too cold (55 degrees of warmth should be the minimum) or even too hot
- unsafe flooring (torn carpets, possibly slippery surfaces)
- exits unmarked or poorly marked
- uncomfortable work stations (service desks, office accommodation etc) and tasks which are physically beyond your people (especially lifting)
- staircases without handrails
- fire risks – and what to do about them.

While most readers will probably consider this list (which is not intended to be exhaustive) rather obvious – and not applicable to their place of work – some of the items do need frequent checking, and this is the point of hazard spotting. This should be carried out by the manager and diarised – but can also form part of one of your regular staff training sessions. More eyes and heads may spot potential risks which escape the manager, but this should not be seen as a reason to make unreasonable demands; the original Act emphasises the importance of being reasonable about all risks.

The following 'Lesson Plan' could form the basis of a training session.

Lesson Plan

SUBJECT **HAZARD SPOTTING**

AIM To give staff practical exercises in spotting potential hazards and to familiarise them with preventative safety procedures

PREPARATION Warn/make arrangements with any other people involved in the company, i.e. department managers, warehouse staff, etc. Do your own hazard spotting at the same time as group!

Main Talking Points:

1 Safety can be divided into three sections

a) safety of people

b) safety of workplace

c) safety of work method

Other Points:

- Responsibility to people
- Learn to check as a matter of course
- Take care in handling machines & electricity
- Don't let habit make you careless

Hazard spotting exercise:

2 a) Brief group as to where in firm they are checking for hazards. Remind them of the sort of thing to look for.

2 b) Discuss hazards spotted during exercise.

Identify:

a) Hazards that group can correct themselves
b) Hazards which must be reported to more senior staff
c) What action should be taken to prevent recurrence.
d) Follow up action necessary, e.g. reporting to supervisor when a hazard is spotted.

Your company may have instituted a Health and Safety audit procedure and the Safety Inspection Summary shown opposite illustrates the range of items which might well be checked in such an audit.

SAFETY INSPECTION SUMMARY

BRANCH ______________________

INSP. BY ______________________

DATE ______________________

	Area/room	Area/room	Area/room	Area/room	Area/room	Area/room
Housekeeping						
Floors/ gangways/ entrances						
Corners, etc.						
Counter glass and area						
Tables, stands, chairs						
Skips						
Fixed machines						
Offices and canteens						
Toilets and lockers						
Manual handling						
Mechanical handling						
Personal protective eqpt.						
Doors, windows, fire exits						
Unsafe acts						
Notices/ rules						
Vehicles						
Electrical equipment						
Additional remarks						

Any business may be visited by an Inspector of the Health and Safety Executive or your local Council, whose task it is to enforce the law, and you must co-operate with them. They are entitled to visit firms without any prior warning.

So, Health and Safety is an important topic – to be taken seriously by everyone. All line managers especially need to have a clear understanding of their firm's policies and procedures!

5. Accidents

Your firm must have an accident book – in which it is important to record any accidents which happen to staff or customers. Most incidents, of course, will (hopefully) be very minor but, as many 'victims' know, the repercussions of accidents often take some time to show up – making it all the more important that a detailed record exists of what occurred.

The secondary purpose of the accident book is to provide the basis for subsequent investigation:

- What actually occurred, and the nature of the accident,
- The unsafe acts and conditions which contributed to the accident,
- What people did, or failed to do,

Resulting in:

- Recommendations on the action which should be taken to prevent a recurrence.

Your team should have been trained in the reporting of accidents and the following sample Lesson Plan may be helpful with this:

Lesson Plan

SUBJECT	**REPORTING OF ACCIDENTS**
AIM	To ensure that, if an accident occurs, staff can follow correct reporting procedure
PREPARATION	Have available a copy of firm's Accident Report form. Be fully aware of company accident reporting procedure.

Main talking points	**Other points**
1 Sometimes accidents will happen to staff or customers	Need to remain vigilant to try to prevent.
2 What do you do if an accident occurs	a) Reporting procedure b) Where first aid assistance can be obtained c) Identify people who can give first aid help
3 Accident Report Form	
Discuss firm's Accident Report Form in detail.	Where to find it, who should fill it in - why it is filled in.

6. Fire!

Fire is probably the biggest risk retailers face – not because of any inherent risk of fires starting of their own accord, but because of the flammability of most of the materials (merchandise) which are stored in retail premises.

Again, the business should have adopted standard procedures in the event that a fire should break out and it is the manager's responsibility to ensure that staff understand their role in these procedures – for example:

- the company's fire drill – what to do if you discover a fire
- how to tackle the fire safely
- the firm's fire fighting equipment and how it should be used
- how and when to evacuate the premises
- how and where to assemble staff and visitors
- the role of fire wardens.

Lesson Plan

SUBJECT — **FIRE PROCEDURE 1**

AIM — To encourage staff to have a conscientious attitude to fire prevention.

PREPARATION — Check knowledge of company's fire prevention methods and any other relevant facts.

Flip chart and marker pens.

Main Talking Points	Other points
1 What are main causes of fires? Discuss with group and list all possible causes.	Unauthorised/ careless smoking Electrical. Flammable liquids. Carelessness.
2 What the company does to prevent fire. Discuss with Group	Fire detection and sprinkler systems. Fire doors and staircases. Layout of departments (customers always within 100 ft of emergency exit). Electrical inspections, rewiring. Good house-keeping rules, Fire Drills, etc. Regular maintenance of all equipment & machinery.
3 What can you do? Discuss with staff and list action to be taken.	Develop a safety attitude. Take care with smoking, cleaning solvents, display material, rubbish, good housekeeping, etc. Report potential hazards when spotted.

Once again, the local Fire Officer is available to give the firm advice about all these factors – but it is normally the responsibility of the company to organise the training of its own staff. Branch or Department group training sessions provide the ideal opportunity.

7. Bomb threats

Mercifully, these hazards are rather less frequent but it is still important that the firm has adopted a formal procedure for handling such threats – just because an incident has never occurred in your business, it does not mean it never will!

Here are three simple checklists illustrating steps which need to be taken in the event of a bomb warning.

Checklist A: Bomb threats

If something suspicious is found:

- Do not touch it
- Call the police on 999
- Ensure the person calling is there to talk to the police.

Anyone receiving a telephoned bomb threat can prevent loss of life and help police track down the terrorists by implementing the following Home Office procedure (Checklist B below).

Checklist B: Caller questions

A caller should be asked the following questions:

- Where is the bomb now?
- When is it going to explode?
- What does it look like?
- What kind of bomb is it?
- What will cause it to explode?
- Did you place the bomb?
- Why?
- What is your name? Address? Telephone Number?

(The last three questions are unlikely to be answered accurately but should still be asked).

Checklist C: Further steps

- Record the conversation if possible
- Tell the caller which town/district you are answering from
- Take down the exact wording of the threat
- Record the date, time of the threatening call and its length
- Record the time the call is completed
- Where the phone displays the caller's number, write it down
- Try dialling 1471 to find the caller's number
- If necessary inform the building co-ordinator
- Ring the police on 999 and record the time of the call
- Note down caller details: Sex, Nationality, Age, How well spoken, Irrational/incoherent/foul, Is it a taped message?
- Was the caller calm, angry, nasal, slurred, crying, excited, stuttered, disguised, slow or rapid; lisping, accented, deep, familiar, laughing or hoarse?
- What was in the background – street, domestic or animal noises? Vehicles, crockery, other people, machinery, office equipment, music?

Scotland Yard also have a free, confidential anti-terrorist number: 0800 789 321 for people to call if they have information about possible terrorist activity.

Retailers probably cannot avoid attracting bomb threats, but we can ensure that we implement that we have the right systems in place. The aim should be to minimise damage to people and property by helping the authorities to do their jobs!

8. The manager and the environment

From time to time the manager will become aware of HM Government initiatives designed to protect our environment; current concerns include:

- water conservation
- energy conservation, and
- packaging and disposal of waste.

In each area businesses are being encouraged to build up an awareness of the importance of looking after the country's natural resources and, as a consequence, achieve a reduction in costs.

Retailers may not normally consider themselves to be major users of water but it can be surprising just how much water can be consumed by that leaking tap or frequently flushing urinal. Metered water bills may quickly draw attention to these types of problems (the responsibility for some may lie with the landlord, of course) but this does not avoid the fact that something needs doing!

It has been estimated that the UK could save up to 20% of its generated energy by better insulation and cost saving and, within the constraints of maintaining a comfortable environment (and well-lit merchandise), it is in managers' interests to minimise the power bill. This may be helped by simply ensuring that unnecessary lights are switched off when the area/room is unused.

A more topical pressure is the current European drive to reduce the levels of packaging waste which has to be buried in landfill sites. Re-cycling would obviously be preferable. Packaging made from plastics, metals, paper and glass materials are all covered by new regulations – directly relevant to businesses handling more than 50 tonnes a year and a turnover of £1M (in the year 2,000). Affected businesses will be required to show that they recover at least 38% of their packaging. Some responsibilities will lie with the firm's suppliers but it is in everyone's interest that this initiative is successful.

Successful Sales Managers encourage their teams to adopt a responsible attitude to the local environment – and try to protect resources, minimising waste wherever possible!

9. Summary

This chapter reminds us that it is not possible for our business to exist in a vacuum. As managers we have direct responsibility for the effects our business has on the environment, our staff and the community at large. Mostly, this will just be a matter of exercising common sense at work.

However, it is important that the manager and the whole team is vigilant against all those risks and threats described in this chapter. Serious threats can lead to disruption of business (at best) and a close–down (at worst). Either way, the employment of our team may be threatened – and this in turn may make any recovery even more difficult; downward spirals can get out of control!

So, every manager has a duty to keep up–to–date with all developments in these fields.

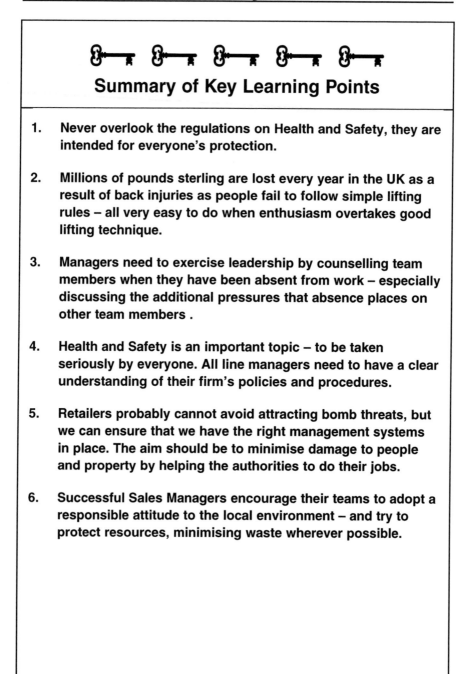

Summary of Key Learning Points

1. Never overlook the regulations on Health and Safety, they are intended for everyone's protection.

2. Millions of pounds sterling are lost every year in the UK as a result of back injuries as people fail to follow simple lifting rules – all very easy to do when enthusiasm overtakes good lifting technique.

3. Managers need to exercise leadership by counselling team members when they have been absent from work – especially discussing the additional pressures that absence places on other team members .

4. Health and Safety is an important topic – to be taken seriously by everyone. All line managers need to have a clear understanding of their firm's policies and procedures.

5. Retailers probably cannot avoid attracting bomb threats, but we can ensure that we have the right management systems in place. The aim should be to minimise damage to people and property by helping the authorities to do their jobs.

6. Successful Sales Managers encourage their teams to adopt a responsible attitude to the local environment – and try to protect resources, minimising waste wherever possible.

FINALE

14

Continuing the Development Process

1. Introduction

This book has blended theory with the best of current practice – there is much that has not been mentioned or covered because, in this growing series, specialist subjects will be covered in much greater depth than has been possible in this broad text. We also hope that readers will be provoked to want to develop their management skills further – after all, the job is possibly the best one in retailing, and really worth doing to the best of our abilities!

This is because:

- line managers can see immediate effects from their efforts,
- the team size is usually small enough to enable rewarding relationships to be developed with individual team members,
- managers can develop their team-working skills in small groups in preparation for larger teams in more senior roles,
- close touch can still be maintained with the firm's customers.

Where else can managers learn so much about what works in management with the 'acid test' so readily identifiable in the eyes of the customer and inside the cash register (or terminal)?

Most senior executives cut their 'management teeth' in departmental or branch management positions and never forget the things they learned from their colleagues, bosses and (most importantly) their staff!

This period will help you too.

In this section, we couple together some simple advice in keeping the development process going – using:

- self-development techniques
- short training courses and
- personal study and reading.

Before exploring each of these items in depth, here is some general advice which should help managers gain maximum results from all the self development effort – especially from the team.

2. Develop your management philosophy

Early chapters emphasised the importance of good leadership techniques to be practised by line managers. The following advice may help in the pursuit of good standards of practice. When the reader stops to think, the checklist will reveal some significant differences between average managers and those who could be described as truly effective.

Checklist: An effective sales manager ...

- Always aims for excellence in customer service.
- Balances concern for the task with concern for teamwork and meeting needs of individuals.
- Gives credit to the team and always talks about Us/We before I/Me and You.
- Takes direct responsibility for team failures rather than allocating blame.
- Maintains high personal integrity.
- Constantly demonstrates positive outlook and enthusiasm for the team and its role.
- Walks and teaches the job on an everyday basis.
- Consults team members regularly and listens carefully to their responses.
- Plans his or her time carefully and uses it as if it is a precious resource.

Checklist (cont)

- Empowers team members to take responsibility for the quality of their own work
- Communicates with team members on both an individual and group basis
- Facilitates performance reviews resulting in meaningful action plans
- Creates great commitment in team members to the organisation and team targets
- Listens actively – rather than talks
- Focuses on vision as well as goals and objectives
- Develops a strong personal presence amongst team members
- Recognises and exploits commercial opportunities.

3. Become a self-developer

There is a great deal we can learn from everyday events – in fact it could be said that, if this does not happen we are unlikely to progress at all.

Learn from your experiences

There are enough people in the world who seem quite incapable of learning from their own experiences – as they simply keep on making the same mistakes!

It is the mark of dedicated 'learners' that this does not happen to them – rather, they keep growing from the experiences they gain on a day-by-day basis.

An enquiring mind is an essential part of this process. Ask yourself:

- What really happened there?
- Why did it occur?
- Who else has had this kind of experience?
- What did they do about it?
- How could I have handled the situation better? With a better result?
- Who might benefit from my experience? And so avoid the same mistakes?

- How will I avoid repeating the undesirable aspects of this experience? and...
- How could I exploit the good aspects?

Discuss management with other experienced managers

Most experienced managers are only too pleased to share some of their experiences with less experienced colleagues; while many might decry their own training skills, most are very keen to help colleagues if this helps overall team performance.

An extension of this advice is to build a 'mentoring relationship' with someone you know and trust who can help you develop your career opportunities. Mentors need not be bosses or even friends; you will probably obtain more objective advice from a former colleague or perhaps from an 'elder statesman' who has already retired.

Mentors advise on all aspects of work, from image matters to negotiating skills and the best ways to sell yourself. Mentors help their 'charges' to seek their own answers to situations – not to solve them the easy way!

Implement your action plans

Action planning is an excellent way of learning from day-to-day situations. Building a personal action plan around challenges experienced in the workplace can provide a valuable agenda for improvement; progressing the plan can then provide a focus for development activities, personal learning and endless 'Post Mortems'!

What is surprising is that key learning points (even those drawn up around menial tasks) may offer valuable progress spread over a period of time. This approach can rapidly mature into a 'Boasting Book' or 'Portfolio' which can be most impressive when attending a promotion interview.

Extract the most you can out of short course opportunities

Most managers are highly committed to their jobs – sufficiently for it to be a struggle to disengage sufficiently for days off – and holidays.

Pressure can also grow if opportunities are offered for managers to attend short courses but, just as holidays help to refresh the spirit, training courses help refresh and develop our knowledge and skills!

It is very important that, when these opportunities are provided, managers grasp them enthusiastically and try their best to 'squeeze' all possible benefits from them.

This may be easier said than done.

For example, short management skills programmes may appear to cover issues in which the manager already has some experience. The question should be asked: 'Could I improve my skills in this area? And would this proposed training experience help to do that? In turn, might that contribute towards better team results – and therefore better achievement against our targets?'

Training can also help us avoid getting stuck in that infamous 'rut'. It is most important for managers to stay 'fresh' and open-minded – especially as new ideas come along (or old ones re-emerge in new clothes)!

It can be easy to reject such ideas – because they represent a 'threat' to what we see as our 'normal' pattern of life. Change can feel like quite a threat to many people.

And then there are all the other 'shadows in the dark' which can present unpleasant threats.

For example - what if I am the only person there who:

- is a man/woman?
- is from my trade sector?
- is under 25 or over 50?
- cannot spell/make a presentation etc?
- is worried about leaving the family?

All these, and other, concerns are perfectly natural but are still not good reasons for not taking up the challenge and gaining from the learning experience!

Your manager, or the person who will sponsor your attendance on this programme, ought to provide you with some pre-course briefing and explain:

- what to expect from the programme
- its objectives and the relevance of the topics covered
- its link to the firm's objectives and strategy
- the learning objectives covered in the programme
- any link with a recent performance review or appraisal you discussed
- the kinds of 'pay-off' which should come from the programme,
- domestic arrangements – e.g. how to travel/where to stay, expenses covered, etc.

This briefing should help to allay many fears and help the participant focus on the key issues involved and, if not provided automatically, can always be requested.

Incidentally, for best results, a detailed briefing ought to be provided by managers for members of their own team whenever they attend course programmes!

4. Towards life-long learning

As we saw in Chapter 5 there are many ways of undertaking training and most are within the reach of all people's pockets. Some countries now encourage employees themselves to make a financial contribution to their own development, and the UK has contributed to this pattern since the development of the Open University and Open College in the 1960's.

We now have a culture in which many managers have grasped the importance of staying ahead through training and development programmes, such as an MBA qualification. This is ironic, as Retailing and Distribution is one of the few industries left where qualifications are not necessarily a pre-requisite to success. Nonetheless, qualification-based courses have a growing importance (and increasing numbers of managers, as students, are taking part in them).

Organisations such as the bssa specialise in providing training programmes for managers in retailing. These vary from self-study, open learning programmes to short courses and residential development schools – and, whilst these are normally sponsored by employers, it is always possible for potential participants to obtain information about them prior to seeking sponsorship. None of these approaches will automatically bring recognition or promotion but they will contribute to maturity and long-term career possibilities.

5. Summary

Self–development is also always possible through reading and this chapter ends with a suggested reading list which will enable determined 'students' to develop their management knowledge and skills further. Each reference will offer the reader further insights into key points referred to in this book and enhance understanding and the opportunities of improving the teams' results through better management insight and ability.

Obtaining consistently good results rarely comes from one or two single steps forward. Rather, we are dependant upon a longer term process which has been described as 'lifelong learning'.

The concept here is that we should consciously invest time in our own development throughout our lives, enabling a continuous improvement of our abilities and results – you do not have to be hugely ambitious to benefit from this process.

Self–development can enable us to handle greater pressure and more difficult trading situations – as well as increasingly complex and demanding management responsibilities.

If this book has helped to awaken readers to opportunities for future development, it will have served a most important purpose. Good luck with all your endeavours; I hope that we have the opportunity to meet on a management workshop in the future!

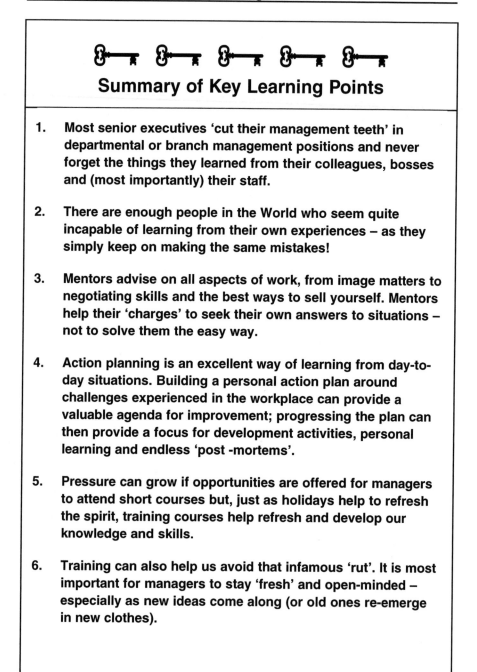

Summary of Key Learning Points

1. **Most senior executives 'cut their management teeth' in departmental or branch management positions and never forget the things they learned from their colleagues, bosses and (most importantly) their staff.**

2. **There are enough people in the World who seem quite incapable of learning from their own experiences – as they simply keep on making the same mistakes!**

3. **Mentors advise on all aspects of work, from image matters to negotiating skills and the best ways to sell yourself. Mentors help their 'charges' to seek their own answers to situations – not to solve them the easy way.**

4. **Action planning is an excellent way of learning from day-to-day situations. Building a personal action plan around challenges experienced in the workplace can provide a valuable agenda for improvement; progressing the plan can then provide a focus for development activities, personal learning and endless 'post -mortems'.**

5. **Pressure can grow if opportunities are offered for managers to attend short courses but, just as holidays help to refresh the spirit, training courses help refresh and develop our knowledge and skills.**

6. **Training can also help us avoid that infamous 'rut'. It is most important for managers to stay 'fresh' and open-minded – especially as new ideas come along (or old ones re-emerge in new clothes).**

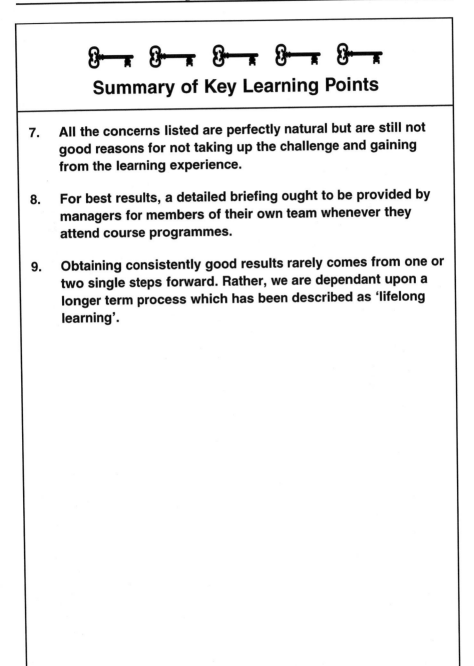

Summary of Key Learning Points

7. All the concerns listed are perfectly natural but are still not good reasons for not taking up the challenge and gaining from the learning experience.

8. For best results, a detailed briefing ought to be provided by managers for members of their own team whenever they attend course programmes.

9. Obtaining consistently good results rarely comes from one or two single steps forward. Rather, we are dependant upon a longer term process which has been described as 'lifelong learning'.

Appendix 1

Recommended reading

Selling and Sales Management

Law for Retailers, Bill Thomas, Management Books 2000, 2003

Retail Selling, Peter Fleming, Management Books 2000, 1995

The Retailer and the Community, Peter Fleming with Karen McColl, Management Books 2000, 2002

Retail Marketing, Peter McGoldrick, McGraw Hill, 1990

A Passion for Excellence, Tom Peters, Collins, 1985

The Profession of Selling (series), John Fenton, Management Books 2000, 2002

The Richer Way, Julian Richer

Retail Buying Techniques, Fiona Elliott and Janet Rider, Management Books 2000, 2003

Leadership and Team-building

The Action-Centred Leader, John Adair, Kogan Page, 1988

Common Sense Leadership, Roger Fulton,Ten Speed Press, 1995

Leadership and the One-minute Manager, K Blanchard, Fontana/ Collins,1988

The One-Minute Manager Builds High Performing Teams, K Blanchard, Harper/Collins, 1996

Positive Leadership, Mike Pegg, Management Books 2000, 1994

The Super Teams Book, Mike Pegg, Management Books 2000, 2003

Team Management, Charles Margerison and Dick McCann, Management Books 2000, 1995

Health and Safety

The A to Z Health and Safety Handbook, Tom O'Reilly, Management Books 2000, 2003

Appendix 3

bssa Courses

The **bssa** provides an annual training programme with the sole aim of developing the competence and skills of retail staff and proprietors. Many of these programmes are complemented by the business book series – the following are particularly relevant.

Retail Law for Managers – the seminar from the book

A one day seminar designed to increase a manager's understanding of the requirements of retail law. This informative programme offers a full briefing on essential statutes and regulations.

Key Topics

- Legal essentials for a contract
- Advertising and display of goods
- Dos and don'ts of price marking
- Trade descriptions – how to avoid 'over-selling'
- Complaints policies – how to handle disputes

Course provider: **PFA International for bssa**

Introduction to Buying – practical training course based on the book: *Retail Buying Techniques*

Delegating responsibility to untrained personnel can feel like giving someone else a blank, but signed, cheque! Buying can be a high-risk activity as the stakes are high.

However, formal training limits the risks of over-stocking and poor merchandise selection, and heightens the chances of increased profits. Buying requires skills – not just flair and creativity!

Key Topics

- Assess strengths and weaknesses of trade and identify sectors of the market

Gather and utilise sales and stock control data on which to plan buying decisions – when and how to order basic stocks

Plan and manage an 'open-to-buy' budget

Build a merchandise range plan and 'model' stocks

Analyse legal and commercial relationships between suppliers, retailers and customers

Negotiate a case with a partner.

Course provider: **PFA International for bssa**

All the above events can also be provided on an In-Company basis – as well as 'open' training events.

Distance Learning – 3 modules

21st Century Selling Skills
This basic six modular sales course is intended to improve the customer service skills and overall efficiency of sales staff whilst emphasising the importance of their role in the business.

21st Century Supervisory Skills
This five modular course is aimed at team leaders and junior managers whose skills need further development for their first managerial appointment enabling them to quickly make a difference in their new role.

Buying & Merchandising Foundation Course
This course is aimed at trainee / assistant buyers or those with buying responsibilities for their company. The manual comprises of 10 modules studied over a 12 month period.

Oxford Summer School – a 7-day Residential School

Supported by the UK's most successful retailers. This premier training programme for middle managers is 'one of the jewels in the crown' of UK retailing. It provides a unique and inspirational experience that challenges and empowers retail managers; enabling them to grow in confidence and to provide them with the motivation to realise their potential.

Challenging case studies based on tutorials culminating in a full scale business exercise based on:

Key Topics:

Leading successful teams.

Stock management and its impact on profits.

Understanding key financial information and its use in enhancing company performance.

Retail store planning and staff costs.

Marketing and Branding and organisation.

Keynote speakers and tutors from the Retail Industry lead this event for bssa.

Oxford Retail Masters Forum

A four day residential course for senior retail managers which is an ideal follow up to the Oxford Summer School.

Objectives:

To provide an understanding of the fundamentals of how a business operates.

To provide an insight into the interpretation and evaluation of the performance of a business.

To examine the challenges facing retailing today and in the future, in terms of economy, consumer, government, city, media, global expansion, technology and innovation.

To develop a clear picture of retailing in the future.

To provide all participants with a wealth of practical ideas that can be taken back into their own business.

The format is a combination of keynote addresses, group study and presentations.

bssa's training programme is constantly being updated and expanded in line with national training developments and requirements.

For further information contact 01295 713391/713389 or visit the website: **www.british-shops.co.uk** and click onto services.

Appendix 3

Other books in this series

RETAIL BUYING TECHNIQUES

Planning, organising and evaluating retail buying decisions and improving profitability

by Fiona Elliott and Janet Rider

(241 pages, £16.99)

For any retailer the acquisition of the right stock at the right price at the right time is crucial to the economic well-being of the business. RETAIL BUYING TECHNIQUES covers every aspect of the all-important buying function. It is packed with case histories and performance tips and will be exceptionally valuable to everyone in the industry with some responsibility for buying.

Subjects covered include:

- Planning the budget
- Planning the structure of the merchandise range
- Developing the product and brands
- Sourcing and buying the product
- Presenting and promoting products profitably

The authors, Fiona Elliott and Janet Rider, are both established retail consultants with extensive experience in buying and merchandising. Between them they have worked for a wide range of companies including well-known retail chains such as Habitat, Owen Owen, British Home Stores, and Co-operative Retail Services as well as a number of smaller specialist companies.

'Good buyers who can build the perfect product range for their market are always in demand ...This book will make an important contribution to the better understanding of any buyer's work, making it essential reading for all executives.'

John Hoerner, Chief Executive, The Arcadia Group

To order this book phone Management Books 2000 on 01285-771441 – credit card orders accepted on Visa or Mastercard, or visit their website - www.mb2000.com.

RETAIL SELLING

How to Achieve Maximum Sales

by Peter Fleming

(220 pages, £16.99)

This is a practical guide for all retail salespeople. It shows you how to improve your sales and increase customer satisfaction.

With more than 100 performance tips, 14 case histories, 16 mini-assignments and 11 self-test questionnnaires, this book is really a complete training course in just 192 pages. Every retail salesperson should have a copy.

Peter Fleming, founder of his own consultancy business, won a major travelling scholarship at the age of 19 on the strength of his sales skills in fashion and household textiles. Graduating into the training profession, he managed the training function in Selfridges and has trained countless sales people and managers through public courses, in-company assignments and training publications.

Here, he shares the successful methods he has learned from frontline experience and case histories of clients, including such companies as BMW, Courts Furnishers, Contessa, Moss Chemists, Dunhill, Equator, Moss Bros., Allders International and Alpha Retail.

'This book gives the sales person a great opportunity to develop key skills which will help them achieve success in this crucial job. I have no hesitation in recommending it to you.'

Tim Daniels, Managing Director, Selfridges

To order this book, phone Management Books 2000 on 01285-771441 – credit card orders accepted on Visa or Mastercard, or visit their website - www.mb2000.com.

LAW FOR RETAILERS

The Legal Beagle keeps you straight with a guide to trading within the law

by Bill Thomas

(236 pages, £12.99 - 2003)

A practical guide for retail managers, salespeople and shop assistants - in fact anyone concerned with the day-to-day business of dealing with retail customers and/or suppliers. The book gives detailed advice on all aspects of retailers' legal obligations to both customers and suppliers, and their possible claims against either in the event of damages, breach of contract etc.

Packed with tips, advice and warnings, the book also contains numerous checklists and procedures to avoid problems in the first place - and practical guidance on how to achieve the best outcome in the event that legal action does become necessary. Subjects covered include:

- Organising your business - the legal rules
- Making and working through a contract
- The problems with credit
- Criminal law on retailing generally, and on food and safety
- Your liability for what you sell
- Due diligence
- Hazard prediction and quality control
- When things go wrong!

'This book is essential reading for everyone in the retail trade. It is a unique guide, charting a practical course through the labyrinth of legal pitfalls and stumbling blocks with which every retailer is familiar. Read this book and you may save yourself a considerable amount of time, money - and worry.'

John Dean, Chief Executive, bssa

To order this book, phone Management Books 2000 on 01285-771441 – credit card orders accepted on Visa or Mastercard, or visit their website – www.mb2000.com.

Index